NOTES FROM
THE
TILT-A-WHIRL

WITHDRAWN

NOTES FROM THE TILT-A-WHIRL

N. D. WILSON

Thomas Nelson
Since 1798

NASHVILLE   DALLAS   MEXICO CITY   RIO DE JANEIRO

Published in Nashville, Tennessee, by Thomas Nelson. Thomas Nelson is a
registered trademark of Thomas Nelson, Inc.

Thomas Nelson, Inc., titles may be purchased in bulk for educational, business,
fund-raising, or sales promotional use. For information, please e-mail
SpecialMarkets@ThomasNelson.com.

Unless otherwise noted, scripture quotations are taken from the King James
Version of the Bible.

Library of Congress Cataloging-in-Publication Data Available Upon Request

ISBN 978-0-8499-6486-2 (RPK)

Printed in the United States of America

13 14 15 16 17 RRD 7 6 5 4 3 2 1

For my sisters
(who have always seen)

CONTENTS

PREFACE

What excuses can I possibly make for this book?

Alcohol was not directly involved. I do not (to my knowledge) have a diseased brain. I've never used drugs. But that's not entirely true. Spring is a drug to me. So is Christmas. Love, poetry, wind, smells, lightning, children, ants, very small beetles —all drugs in their own way.

It's not my fault. Those things made me write this book. Those things and a few others, both sweet and sour.

Here's how it happened: Philosophers of various sizes and shapes and flavors and ages crowded into the saloon of my skull and began throwing elbows to make some space. Poets and preachers piled in with them. John Donne said some zippy things about Kant, and the ancients wouldn't stop snickering at the moderns. On top of that, Gilbert Keith Chesterton (that fabulously large Catholic writer) overheard someone making fun of Milton (it didn't matter that the insults were all true).

Note the eruption.

For me, this book was an occurrence. It rolled over me. I worked to shape and control it, to pace it, to leash it and teach it to sit and roll over. I did my best. But at times my best was insufficient, and in some places you might notice this thing climbing on the furniture, licking my face, or dragging me down the street.

I enjoyed the ride, though it left me panting and clammy. I'm grateful to the thinkers and writers who triggered the brawl. I'm grateful to God for the eyes in my head, and for the wildness of the spinning world these eyes see. This world, shaped by His words, can never be tamed by mine. But there is joy to be had in trying and falling short. My cuts and bruises will heal. I may live long enough to try again.

I've learned from this, and I feel lighter—like I've lost some mental weight. I hope that's a good thing.

A few comments, warnings, and an explanation or two:

This book does not go straight. It is not a road in Wyoming. The earth spins while orbiting the sun. A car on a Tilt-A-Whirl queases children at the county fair using a similar motion—tightly spinning on a larger, also rotating platform (throw in some rising and falling for good measure). This book is built on that pattern—spinning small and spinning big—and follows the earth through the seasons of one orbit. Like the earth and the Tilt-A-Whirl, you will end at a beginning.

This book attempts to find unity in cacophony. The barrage of elements (philosophy, poetry, theology, narrative, *ad nauseam*) may at times feel random. It isn't. It is intended to be symphonic: dissimilar voices and instruments moving from dissonance to harmony. The emotional spectrum (anger, love, happiness, grief) is meant to be as broad as the material covered. It seeks the same unity.

Words: They are more than tools used in the transfer of simple information from mind to mind. Throughout, I was attempting to use them as paint, spreading them on a canvas rather than paper. I wanted to write to the body and to the senses as well as the mind. Did I? It's a tricky goal, and perhaps I shouldn't admit to having aimed so high. The admission can make failure more obvious.

There are times when my word choice may seem odd for a "religious" book hoping to reach a "religious" audience. But rest easy—I never reach the level of shock and surprise achieved by such writers as the prophet Ezekiel.

Rhythm: Given the movement, pace, and shape of this book, I have included occasional seasonal rest stops, hiatuses (hiati, if you really prefer) along the way. This is so no one will pull a hamstring.

Title: In the nineteenth century, Dostoyevsky, the Russian genius, wrote a short novel entitled *Notes from Underground*. My title is an acknowledgment to him and to his vision.

On too many explanations in the front of a book: It is art to conceal art. Yes. I know. Some would say I'm ruining what little artistry exists in this book by including too much direct commentary on it. But I see no greater danger in this preface beyond that of boring a potential reader flipping pages in a bookstore. If artistry exists in the book, then surely it can survive despite a few dull opening pages. (How many people read prefaces?) If no artistry exists, then I have ruined nothing.

At this point, I feel the need to piously admonish all readers to buckle up, as it is the law. But I've forgotten to include seat belts, and I don't know where I left the liability waivers.

Finally, before the true beginning, I would like to thank the makers of Dramamine. My gratitude is real.

WELCOME

I am a traveler.

Do I sound important? Or at least meaningful? I'm not Kerouac. And I'm not in sales. I travel like the flea on a dog's back. I travel unintentionally, a very small cowboy born on a bull. I travel with the Carnival. Where it goes, I go. Its people are my people, and its land is my land. Most of my time is spent on the Tilt-A-Whirl and occasionally in the squirrel cages. I couldn't stop traveling if I tried, and not because of some kind of wanderlust, gypsy blood, a need for meaningful experiences, or a desire to see Europe's castles.

I was born into the Carnival. I've done all my living, sleeping, playing, growing, and throwing up at the Carnival. When I die, I won't escape it—not that I'd want to. Death is that black stripe above my head on the measuring board. When I've reached it, well, then I can go on the gnarly rides.

Just to be clear, I live on a near perfect sphere hurtling through space at around 67,000 miles per hour. Mach 86 to pilots. Of course, this sphere of mine is also spinning while it hurtles, so tack on an extra 1,000 miles per hour at the fat parts. And it's all tucked into this giant hurricane of stars. Yes, it can be freaky. Once a month or so, my wife will find me lying in the lawn, burrowing white knuckles into the grass, trying not to fly away. But most of the time I manage to keep my balance despite the speed, and I don't have to hold on with anything more than my toes.

You live here too. Which means I'm not special. We're all carnies, though some people are in denial. They want to be above it all, above the mayhem of laughter and people and lights and animals and the dark sadness that lurks in the corners and beneath the rides and in the trailers after hours. So they ride the Ferris wheel, and at the top, they think they've left it all behind. They've ascended to a place where they can take things seriously. Where they can be taken seriously.

Let them have their moment. You and I can eat our corn dogs and wait and smile. Solomon smiles with us.

The wheel turns. The earth spins and runs its laps. We all go around.

What the hell *is* this place? Just looking around, I can tell you that whatever is going on, spheres are a theme, and so are insects. We are on a sphere, spinning around a much bigger sphere (which happens to be burning hot enough to singe my face, even at this distance) while other spheres of various sizes do the same thing, and a smaller, sad, little-dead-poet sphere with acne scars spins around us, lighting the night, causing the oceans to heave their bosoms and pant, and increasing violent crime (really). And our blue ball is primarily populated by small things with exoskeletons, no matter how you measure it. Invertebrates outnumber us, outweigh us, out-vary us, and bite us more often than we bite them. If you find yourself a quiet little deciduous forest during the summer, you can sit still and listen to the clatter of their spoor falling into the undergrowth while chiggers creep carefully into your skivs. I have a friend who got some government money for doing just that.

If I were a publisher (which I'm not), and an agent (I wouldn't consider unagented submissions) submitted a proposal for a fantasy taking place in this world, then I would tell him in no uncertain terms that I only handle important stories, realistic stories, stories believable in texture and character, and then I would tell him to try the pulps, maybe aim for a straight-to-paperback grocery store novel, target an audience more likely to believe something so far-fetched—an audience less likely to have college degrees. In that pitched fantasy world, the spheres would be so perfectly aligned that when the moon passed in front of the sun, the two would be identically sized. And when the earth's shadow fell on the moon's face, it also would be perfectly sized to brown the moonlight. Yeah, right. Whatever. A bit contrived, don't you think? Perfect balls? Some flaunting tutus? Come now. Show some respect for my intelligence.

What is this place? *Why* is this place? Who approved it? Are the investors happy? The stockholders? Was this cosmic behavior expected? Am I supposed to take it seriously? How can I? I've watched goldfish make babies, and ants execute earwigs. I've seen a fly deliver live young while having its head eaten by a mantis. And I had a golden retriever that behaved like one.

This is not a sober world. A mouse once pooped on my toddler nephew, provoked by traps in the living room. Misled by board books, my nephew identified the offending rodent as a sheep. Bats really do exist. Caterpillars really turn into butterflies—it's not just a lie for children. Coal squishes into diamonds. Apple trees turn flowers into apples using sunlight and air.

I've seen a baby born. And, *ahem*, I know what made it. But I'm not telling. You'd never believe me.

There are various theories as to how and why this all happened, attempts at explaining the sheer number of creeping things in the world, the stars, the life cycle of frogs, the social behavior of fish, the meaning of love, life, and a really good hamburger. But in order to know why this is all here, a simple *how* is a prerequisite. How did this place happen? I live here, so it shouldn't be too hard to figure it out.

Call in the suspects. Make them line up, turn sideways, and wait impassively while we look them over. But before you do, one thing should be made perfectly clear. There can be no easily believable explanation for everything I've seen in this little ball-happy universe of ours. Occam's well-worn razor will do us no good. There will be no "simplest" explanation. A single world combining galaxies, black holes, Jerry Seinfeld, over 300,000 varieties of beetle, Shakespeare, adrenal glands, professional bowling, and the bizarre reproductive patterns of wasps (along with teams of BBC cameramen to document them), precludes easily palatable explanations.

A neutral observer would not find this world to be believable. Ergo, the cause of said unbelievable world must place similar stretch marks on the imagination.

Step forward, please. Turn to the left.

If I were an Apache Indian, I would tell you a story about the Creator rubbing his eyes as if long asleep and rousing himself to shape the world. He began with friends. When there were four of them, they clasped hands; the sweat mingled and dropped out in the shape of a ball. They kicked it around, and the wind helped it expand until it had grown into our world. For all I know, they're kicking it still. That the creative moment also served as the invention of soccer is a clever use of resources.

If I were Hawaiian, the story would be about a love triangle, fury, despair, and a volcano's revenge.

My Norse fathers (I'm sure there were some) understood that the world was a cold, hard, and depressing place. At the beginning, there had to be an evil ice giant, chopped up by Odin and his brothers. They recycled his flesh, using it to create the world.

Or try this: In the beginning, there was only an egg, laid in or on or through chaos. After thousands of years, it hatched and out came Pangu, the creator. Pangu divided Yin from Yang, the earth from the heavens, and eventually, he laid himself down and his body became creation, divvying things up nicely—hair into stars, breath into wind, eyes into sun and moon. All of his parasites crawled off and became people. Which, given the history of civilization, isn't too hard to believe.

Babylonians would get Marduk on stage, along with much begetting of monsters and the gutting of his goddess mother.

There are a lot more. I could behave myself, become academically cautious (no fear of that), and we could walk through one after the other, each expounded thoroughly along with all of its variations. We could get into African, Mayan, and Australian aboriginal versions, along with a few dozen others. Or we could move right on to the pervasive themes, those things that manage to crop up time and time again—order versus chaos, violent overthrow and creation by means of recycled dead, lots of blood, struggling gods, misguided affection, and serious divine parenting issues. But even those don't really get to the root, the common human itchiness when it comes to existence.

First, every culture has felt the overwhelming pressure of existence itself and the need to explain it. There's a sort of nervousness apparent in the myths of every people group, as if maybe we're not supposed to be here and we all have to rehearse our story before the authorities come.

"We're sorry . . . there was this ice giant," we explain.

"When Pangu died, we had nowhere else to go," we tell the cop.

"Don't you like soccer?" we ask the judge.

Second, we don't just feel the need to explain and justify

existence, we also seem to understand that our explanation needs to be as outlandish as ourselves, as impossible as reality. This is no time for dogs eating homework. This requires some serious imaginative effort. Personable dragons, wind-inflated worlds and carcasses, dying wolves, cosmic blood, divine urine, exploding gas, and an ever-expanding universe—pick your cast of characters and create your own mythology. *Explain* yourself. Justify your presence here, the presence of the world. Even harder, explain the world's personality. Find a single seed to account for it all. Sit by a campfire, or in a college lab, and spin your tale. Compete with the choir of old stories. Sign up your devotees and acolytes. Sculpt yourself something out of clay, add some odd anatomical detail, and convince yourself that it needs a bowl of fruit, or a goat, or maybe the volcano needs a virgin, or Zeus needs a shepherd girl (again). Or get a degree in philosophy, and ride that Ferris wheel. Look down at the Carnival, be safely above our madly spinning world, the mountains, thunderheads birthing lightning while they roll, the smell of lawn clippings and fresh-cut cedar. Hide behind big words, or listen to a child's first laugh and know that this world is here, that you are in it, and that its flavors are deep and layered and its lights are bright. Know that it's real.

Welcome to Carnival. Ride the wheel back down. Come out from the shadows and lopsided trailers. There's a story to tell, a world of surprises and questions to explore, a personality often searched for to be unearthed and understood in the reality around us. And there's someone behind it, uncomfortable answers to the hows and whys and whats.

In the beginning was the Word, and the Word was with God, and the Word was God. Through Him were all things made.

Welcome to His poem. His play. His novel. Skip the bowls of fruit and statues. Let the pages flick your thumbs.

This is His spoken world.

TICKETS, PLEASE

Winter—the spinning begins.

Snow is so overused. One sentimental, overly structured ice flake might have some value. But God never seems capable of moderation or of understanding the basic concepts behind supply and demand. He constantly devalues His own products. Give me one flake, a cool room, and a magnifying glass and I will admire its artistry. But right now, I'm sitting by my window on a Christmas night, staring out at winter wastefulness in the extreme. Miles of clouds, clouds larger than states, have turned into crystal stars and now streak silently past my window to their deaths. Well, not quite silently. The stars are falling fast enough that if you step outside, like I just did, you can hear the whisper of collisions and delicate frozen impacts, each six-pointed perfection complaining as it arrives—

"They told me I was special. There's two and a half bazillion of us in this hedge and more falling. Does anyone here care about overpopulation? A market crash? Close the sky. Lobby for a moratorium."

But the storm-whispers sound more pleased to me. Excited even—

"I knew I was different from the rest of you plebes. Look how silly and gothic you all look with your skinny, knobbed arms. I'm unique. Neoclassical."

Try counting the flakes. Really count them. I'll step back outside for a quick estimate. Let's be conservative. Assuming that we're in the middle of this storm and it only stretches ten miles in each direction (*Ha*, says the weather man), and assuming that the storm is a tiny one hundred feet tall, and skipping the preexisting ground accumulation, and eyeball estimating the frenzied blizzard's air content at a meager ten flakes per cubic foot, then we are looking at about ... 11,151,360,000,000 flakes in the air above a small patch in Idaho at one particular moment on Christmas night at the end of the year 2007. Just this storm, this tiny little slice of winter could divvy out seventeen hundred flakes to every person on this planet. More impressively, that number has the US national debt beat by trillions.

I look out my window at the proud Christmas tumble. Ye flakes, do you care what I think? Hearken to my insults: You're totally devalued—like stars and galaxies and insect species. For all your balance and your beauty and your impossible symmetry, you're each not even worth a buck. Or a cent. If I could get a penny for each of you, then I'd make the *Forbes* rich-people list (somewhere below the Wal-Mart heirs).

We all know that each flake is different and unique, because we've all been to preschool. Each one is beautiful, yeah, yeah, we know that too. But how can we possibly value these things when their maker slings them around like so much trash? Actually, I've never seen anyone sling this much trash. Doesn't He realize that people will curse this tomorrow? That they'll shovel it and salt it and SUV it into gray slop? Does He know that my daughters are going to roll in it, melting thousands of flakes with their flushed cheeks and tens of thousands with their tongues?

Dogs are going to pee on this stuff in the morning. They're probably getting down to it right now.

So begins a new year, a new solar lap.

◆

Philosophers have long marveled at the world. But that's not exactly accurate. Some philosophers have marveled. Most have responded to the overwhelming weight of reality with pontification and soft-boiled verbiage. The rest have just whined about what a terrible, hard, godless world it is. The world hurts their feelings, and so they fire back dissertations full of insults— calling it an accident, pointless, a derivative of chaos, occasionally even going so far as to deny its existence. But the world doesn't care. It has thick skin, and all the most important thinkers have become part of it.

Should we care about philosophers when the world so

clearly doesn't? Should we bother to remember the names and ideas of men who may live on as nothing more than a headache to college freshmen everywhere?

Why wouldn't we want to? We name our diseases—interesting or no. We name schools of architecture. We name every novel, every play, every food, every ride at the county fair. These men felt burdened by our existence. They worked to justify and explain (or destroy) our presence in this universe, our communication, our ethics, our knowledge. They felt the need for a centuries-long game of intellectual Twister, and they've ruined many things. Doesn't that make them important enough to remember? Like the chicken pox, each of them happened only once. Like the common cold, they build on each other and mutate. If you've been to college, you've heard of them. If you live in the western world, you've played by their rules.

Plato, the first true pope of philosophy (sorry, Socrates), argued for a World of Forms above this reality—a transcendent plane of perfect essences, pure and lovely, where nothing ever gets muddy (including the essence of mud). No football. Many Christians today still think of Heaven in a sort of default, platonic way, and somehow manage to look forward to an existence in a cloudy, spiritual world busy with harps, and nothing much to do.

Aristotle snitched Plato's pure, untainted essences and crammed one inside each particular object on our own plane of material existence. My desk no longer partakes of platonic deskness in the sky, but is somehow inhabited by pure, inner deskness —and it is that internal purity that all desks share; it is that which makes them desks. My backache (when you get all the way down to its essence) is pure and perfect and ideal. If that sounds stupid, don't admit it. *Mui importante, sî?* Just nod and try to look sage and a little conflicted. They'll still give you your degree.

Plato wasn't the only pre-Christian Greek to inform Christian assumptions and mind-sets. Aristotle has maintained virtual sainthood among many religious academics through the centuries. The theology behind the Catholic Mass hung on Aristotle. The unimportant, accidental exteriors of the bread and the wine remain the same; it's that perfect, hidden essence that has been replaced. The material surface is irrelevant. On that inner Aristotelian level, the bread gains the essence of flesh and the wine the essence of blood.

The default mind-set behind the evangelical concept of conversion can often become more than a little Greekish as well.

Skipping centuries to the modern Enlightenment, Descartes, the Frenchman, had a little trouble knowing that he existed. But then he looked to the Little Engine That Could and learned that all he needed to do was think that he was, and he would be. *Cogito, ergo sum.* I think, therefore I am. Say it often enough, be willing to help out other trains in trouble, and you'll be fine. I think I am. I think I am. Descartes *cogitoed* himself (and the rest of the world) into being. Because of the mental ace he found in his mental sleeve, the modern world was built. Its foundation? Reason can get you anywhere.

Leibniz, a bit of a Boy Scout, thought this world had to be the best of all possible worlds (since a perfect God could create no less). Easy enough.

Voltaire made good fun of him. Even easier.

Immanuel Kant wrote books with words like *prolegomena* in the title and thought morality was dependent upon (and monitored by) the ethereal laws of logic.

Aztecs thought they had to rip the hearts out of living victims on top of ziggurats if they wanted the sun to keep coming up.

Shingles is a rash caused by the same virus that causes the chicken pox.

A pig in a blanket is a hot dog wrapped in dough and baked.

A Tilt-A-Whirl is one of the few carnival rides that appears to follow a random pattern of motion. Free-spinning cars are mounted on a spinning (and tilting) platform. It was invented in the 1920s. You can buy your own for under half a million.

Heidegger was a Nazi. Can you think of a better reason to pay him no mind?

Wittgenstein was a beery swine (according to the authorities in the Monty Python brain trust). I can't believe it. Beeriness would have made him more readable.

Nietzsche—a weak, but strongly mustachioed, Lutheran pastor's son—defined evil (in *The Antichrist*) as "whatever springs from weakness."

David Hume, the Scot, (*knowingly*) declared God and knowledge impossible without any apparent sense of irony.

French existentialists, wise men all and examples to philosophers everywhere, killed themselves.

Give me priests. Give me men with feathers in their hair or tall domed hats, female oracles in caves, servants of the python, smoking weed and reading palms. A gypsy fortune-teller with a foot-pedal Ouija board and a gold fishbowl for a crystal ball knows more about the world than many of the great thinkers of the West. Mumbling priests swinging stink cans on their chains and even witch doctors conjuring up curses with a well-buried elephant tooth have a better sense of their places in the world. They know this universe is brimming with magic, with life and riddles and ironies. They know that the world might eat them, and no encyclopedia could stop it.

I am a hypocrite. I grant it readily. I have read the philosophers (not all of them, thank God). I've been tested on the philosophers. I'll talk about the philosophers, but watch my lip. It curls when I do. I hope I'm untainted. Every four years I'll watch figure skating, but I'm no closer to buying myself tights.

Marx called religion an opiate, and all too often it is. But philosophy is an anesthetic, a shot to keep the wonder away.

What is the world? What kind of place is it? What is it doing? Why is it here? How do we know? The questions are fine. Sophia is the goddess of wisdom. *Philosophia*—the brotherly love of wisdom—is a perfectly clean pastime for boys and girls alike. But philosophy proper has become a place to hide, a place to pursue immortality (through never going out of print) by being foggy enough that room is always left for discussion—for future dissertations.

Huzzah for questions. Nobody reasonable dislikes them in moderation. But does anyone actually want answers? Is the journey the destination? Please, no. Let me out of your Volkswagen bus at the next corner. Would a successful answer constitute failure? If you knew the meaning of life, would you necessarily like it?

Medieval alchemists had a tangible goal, and when they all died of lead poisoning, posterity could see that they had failed. Contemporary philosophers work to avoid tangible goals and wallow in the sauna of thought. Apply with strong enough reference letters, and you can too. Pay them enough money and they'll turn Nietzsche loose on your freshman child.

Exception: Socrates had his moments (though it would have been difficult to spend a Saturday with him). His greatest achievement in a tasteful nutshell: "All that I know is that I know nothing." Everyone likes an honest man. But it didn't really stop him from talking. At least if Plato is to be believed.

What is the world? A large (compared to most malls), moist, inhabited, spinning ball. What kind of place is it? The round kind. The spinning kind. The moist kind. The inhabited kind. The kind with flamingos (real and artificial). The kind where water in the sky turns into beautifully symmetrical crystal flakes sculpted by artists unable to stop themselves (in both design and quantity). The kind of place with tiny, powerfully jawed mites assigned to the carpets to eat my dead skin as it flakes off. The kind with sharks, and nose leeches, and slithery parasitic things (with barbs) that will swim up you like a urinary catheter if only you oblige by peeing in a South American river. The kind with people who kill and people who love and people who do both. The kind with people who think water from the Ganges is good for them and people who think eating the heart of their enemy will ward off death, and others who think they can cure their own failing brains if only they harvest enough uncommitted cells from human young.

This world is beautiful but badly broken. St. Paul said that it groans, but I love it even in its groaning. I love this round stage where we act out the tragedies and the comedies of history. I love it with all of its villains and petty liars and self-righteous pompers. I love the ants and the laughter of wide-eyed children encountering their first butterfly. I love it as it is, because it is a story, and it isn't stuck in one place. It is full of conflict and darkness like every good story. And like every good story, there will be an ending. I love the world as it is, because I love what it will be.

I love it because it spins and tilts, because it's dizzying, because of the night sky and the swirling lights.

But I have run too far ahead. We should be more . . . philosophical.

Disclaimer: If you think the world is flat, I am not here to convince you otherwise. If you think the world is meaningless rubbish bobbing in the galactic culvert of accidental reality, I don't intend to grapple with your ever-so-subtle epistemological claims. I am here to paint you a picture of the world I see.

I have a clumsy brush, and my tongue sticks out the corner of my mouth. I've even put a shirt on backward like a priest. I hope they're not offended.

And now let's find Sophia and give her a little lovin'. Brotherly-like.

◆

If we hope to answer such grand sweeping questions as "What is the meaning of existence?" and "What determines good and evil?" and "Who am I?" and "Is it all right to park illegally?" then we should start with something a little more basic, something that even scientists should be able to answer.

What is the world made of?

There are a number of proposed answers floating around out there already. The world, according to more than a few gentlepeople in orange robes, is an illusion. What is the illusion made of? Mostly suffering.

George Berkeley, an eighteenth-century bishop, gave a similar answer. The world exists within the mind of God. We and this and everything hold our ontology (being) within His imagination. Berkeley denied the material nature of the universe entirely. We're thoughts. Nothing but thoughts.

Samuel Johnson, upon first hearing this new philosophy, exuberantly kicked a large rock, saying, "I refute it thus!" Sore toes are a compelling argument.

Of course, the ancients broke the world down to four elements—earth, air, fire, and water. Fair enough, but what are *they* made of?

I could buy a picture book entitled *What Is the World Made Of?* but I don't think it would get me past solids, liquids, and gases—our restatement of the ancient formulation (excluding fire as energy).

We built a periodic table, laughed at the ancients for being so simplistic, and named a barrage of elements. Elements are supposed to be things that are elemental—things that won't break down any further. Things like gold? Lead? Sodium? Californium? But those things have nuclei and electrons and other smaller, trickier bits of business.

Some contemporary thinkers start talking about dimensions, cosmic silly string, and other postulated unmeasurables. Einstein gave us space-time and a whole lot of bad sci-fi along with it.

The current, most cutting-edge mystics in physics departments around the world know the answer. Go to one of the research labs, get a sticker name tag, and hitch yourself to a perky cosmic tour guide.

What is the world made of?

Well, it's simple. Most of what you see around you is made of up quarks, down quarks, and leptons. Now you know. (And if you would only spend more time online, I wouldn't have to tell you these things.)

Are we allowed to ask what quarks are made of? Can I Google that? How about leptons?

The perky one continues: Quarks and leptons are very, very tiny, and when bonded together in different arrangements, they make up reality around us. We can't vouch for the farthest reaches of distant space.

What are they made of?

The four types of bond that keep reality from flying apart

like a microwaved egg are as follows: strong, weak, electro-magnetic, and gravitational.

Strong? That's all they know? Don't we need a more im-pressive name if we're talking about bonding fundamental reality?

Most of what you see is actually empty space, or nothing-ness. The combined volume of the most basic material particles that make up something like a chair is only a tiny fraction of the volume of the chair itself as you see it spatially extended in front of you.

Nice. What are quarks made of?

Did you know that scientists once thought the cell was made out of plum pudding?

Yes, I did. Seems reasonable. What's a lepton made of?

Recently scientists have created the blackest substance in the world. It absorbs 99.9% of light.

What are quarks made of?

The next tour will focus on antimatter. It begins in fifteen minutes. Please visit the gift shop. And remember, we are avail-able for parties.

I have no trouble at all believing in the existence of quarks. I'm told they are subatomic particles that make up protons and neutrons. I'm also told that no single quark has ever been suc-cessfully isolated, and that they have no identifiable components. Which means that they are themselves and are made from noth-ing but themselves. At least until we get better microscopes or learn to speak electron. But why are we talking about this?

Let's run through what we know.

I have an olive on my desk. It is a product of Spain. It was grown on a tree. Which means that the chlorophyll in the olive leaves absorbed energy from sunlight and used that energy to attack the air. Carbon was harvested from carbon dioxide, the oxygen was released back into the lungs of Spanish children, and the carbon was shaped into leaves and bark and this olive. Like me, the olive is carbon-based. It is made of cells, which are made of molecules, which are made of atoms, which are (as we all now know) made of quarks and leptons, which are . . .

The options are limited, but all of them present a problem. First, maybe quarks really are elemental. What are they made of? Themselves. Second, maybe they have components that we haven't identified. In which case, what are those new components made of? Other components? What are those made of? Infinite regress isn't possible. The world cannot be resting on the back of a purple turtle on the back of a purple turtle on the back of a purple turtle on the back of a purple turtle on the back of a purple turtle . . . It doesn't even help if you work in antiturtles.

Here is the moment of my amaze. The olive that I hold in my hand along with its friendly minced pimento, this olive that I now taste and eat, that former olive was, on some level, made out of something that was . . . *not made from anything*.

There is another word for *not anything*. The word is nothing. At some point, that is the answer to the question. What is it made of? What is it made of?

Nothing. And yet . . . it is.

But Samuel Johnson is still right and Berkeley is still wrong.

That olive had mass, it had savor and flavor, texture and temperature, and even a tiny fragment of pit that nicked my gum. It had a measurable amount of potential energy. I am comfortable saying that the olive was no illusion. That the material world exists in all of its toe-stubbing glory. (I see no reason to wander down the long, lonely road of self-sensory doubt. That way avoids no difficulties and only leads to chat rooms, meds, atonal music, and cosmic loathing. It is a slow and painful suicide. And, in my opinion, it's tacky.)

We have come this far using only the sense our mothers gave us. Do we agree that matter, that my olive, cannot be the top of a material tower, an infinite, inverted pyramid that stretches downward, ever downward, with no first floor, no foundation, and ultimately no ground? If we do, then three real options still wait on us. Bring them out; they've all been called Sophia before. Let them walk the runway, and we'll see which one moves more fluidly, more intuitively. Which is the most beautiful and has the best birthing hips? Which could have mothered such a world as ours?

One is truth, and shapes the world. One we will call truth, and it will shape how we see the world. It would be nice if they overlapped.

Sophia 1: *Matter* is actually infinite. Where the regress stops, there is some physical element that is made from nothing else and . . . has always had existence.

This is the atheistic evolutionary story. The universe consists only of time and chance acting on matter. At some point, the ancient matter blew up, and now here we are.

Sophia 2: Something *immaterial* is infinite, has always had existence, and at some point created the material world.

Ooh, I like her. Every little thing she does is magic.

Sophia 3: Blend. There is some *material* in the world that has always had existence, and there is something *immaterial* that has always had existence.

This is actually the creation story of most theistic and polytheistic religions. A god grabs hold of fluxing chaos, or their offspring, or their own thigh, or something with prior existence and reshapes it into the world around us. Norse, Greek, Aztec, and even Muslim creations begin this way.

Of course, any number of flavors and stories fit into these categories, particularly the last one. People and peoples have watched the stars and made their choice, shaping themselves and their cultures in doing so. The choice is not a question of logic, though we may make it logically. We cannot boost logic to the level of a transcendent arbiter here. It cannot whisper the answer in our ear. Any knowledge at this level, at this fundamental question of origins and ultimate metaphysics, must come through something else.

Welcome to the world of faith.

Here is my lady, my picture, my philosophical account of an olive. I look around at the stuff of the world and I ask myself what it is made of.

Words. Magic words. Words spoken by the Infinite, words so potent, spoken by One so potent that they have weight and mass and flavor. They are real. They have taken on flesh and dwelt among us. They are us. In the Christian story, the material world came into existence at the point of speech, and that speech was *ex nihilo*, from nothing. God did not look around for some cosmic goo to sculpt, or another god to dice and recycle. He sang a song, composed a poem, began a novel so enormous that even the Russians are dwarfed by its heaped up pages.

You are spoken. I am spoken. We stand on a spoken stage. The spinning kind. The round kind. The moist kind. The kind of stage with beetles and laughter and babies and dirt and snow and fresh-cut cedar.

You are made of cells. I am made of cells. My cells are built on molecules. My molecules make use of atoms. My atoms are mostly space, but the bits that aren't are called quarks. My quarks are standing because they're obedient. They've been told to by a Voice they cannot disobey.

For Berkeley and Buddhists and most breeds of Hindu, this world is illusory, sleight of hand. It seems material, the way the smoke plays with the mirrors, but it isn't. The world is Vegas magic. Pick a card.

Kick a stone. There are no tricks here. There are no props, no prefabbed white rabbits. The magic is real, and I stand blinking on the stage because of it. I'm real. I'm heavy. I'm matter. Cut me and I'll bleed. But I'm not made out of anything, and if the Magician, the Poet, the Word, if the Singer were to stop His voice, I would simply cease to be.

It's cold tonight, and my mind is too small to grasp the world, tired from trying. I could walk back outside and stare at the stars, those tiny, twinkling, huge, spherical firestorms, but more clouds have rolled in behind the blizzarding herd that only just left.

Tomorrow, according to the weather prophet, these clouds will crystallize and turn into six-pointed haiku, haiku like you've never seen, each subtly different, each capturing a different mood, a different beauty. Each priceless, a divine word.

If I were infinite, I could read and love each one. I could remember the dance of each flake since the world was born.

But I'm not infinite. And so I keep a shovel for when the haiku falls, a bag of salt to fend off the whispering storm.

BREATHING CHARACTERS

I stand on a jetty with my face toward the storm—the Pacific at its winter angriest. Waves tear at the man-made point, unwearying, supported by the wind. Water darts sting my face, whipped down from the sky and up from the sea. They come with the same bite, allies, but the rain is fresh and sweet. The spray salts my lips.

My wife has spent more time with the sea. This is her ocean. She is huddled behind the lighthouse, calling for me. I am less afraid. Perhaps foolish. She knows more faces now among the dead.

Is this what mortality means? Is this how I know my body is of the sort that can stop, that can feed crabs, that will someday be placed in a box and dropped in a hole? I have a need to stand near the edge, to feel this small risk, to feel my heart beat.

If I were not the dying sort, I would be standing closer, beneath the full blow of each breaker.

The ocean spreads to the horizon, and while the wind gusts and the waves crash, they are nothing compared to what this beast can do. The ocean is only playing, licking the feet of a continent, itching to play rougher.

There are shellfish fossils in the Rockies.

Yesterday the power was out thanks to this winter storm. Spray climbed cliffs and crossed roads. I loaded my children in the car and, along with hundreds of other mortals, drove them down to look at the angry sea, caged by continents.

They laughed until the doors opened, and then they stepped outside and cried. I showed them how to turn their backs to the wind, how to lean against it, but the rain stung and bit, even through my jeans. Back inside the car, they laughed again.

I have seen a picture of a tsunami rumbling down an Asian street. People are running, tiny in front of the towering filthy water, but not so tiny that their faces are hidden—smiling faces, faces wide in laughter.

That wave was a killer. Those faces have found other uses in the dust.

"Come back!" my wife yells. I turn and look at her. She's still smiling, laughing in the lighthouse lee.

"I have life insurance!" I shout. "I'm fine."

She grimaces.

I watch another wave claw at the stone and stick out my tongue to taste its death.

She waits for me. I hurry now, and my wet hand finds hers out of the wind. Our kiss tastes like potato chips.

We are alive. We are here, in this part of a story, standing by the sea, laughing under a surly sky.

We are cold, but not so cold as the dead.

How many quarks are out there, splashing around in this storm? How many vowels are in a hurricane? This wet strength, so enormous beside our small arms, is itself only a tiny corner of the spoken world, a tiny corner of this poem. Bigger breakers swirl in Jupiter's eye, but who sees them? Stars and worlds twist in solar storms. This storm is nothing, and I am less. But to an infinite artist, a Creator in love with His craft, there is no unimportant corner, there is no thrown-away image, no tattered thread in the novel left untied.

This ocean, tiny in the universe, is here because it's beautiful. This word, these words that keep surging and crashing and grinding against the contrast of cliffs, they are strong and guttural, like the taste of Anglo-Saxon. This is poetry, but it is not delicate and fragile, a placid ocean beneath a Bible verse on an inspirational poster.

This poetry has testicles. It's rougher than rodeo. Which is why the cliffs are crowded with spectators.

◆

Looking out through the lens of true *ex nihilo* creation—at a spoken world—everything becomes an artistic touch. Every crack in the plaster, every bathroom-dwelling spider, looks out at me like a stage prop, an author's added texture, a fellow character living at this time, inhabiting the same paragraph that I do.

There are Christians in the world who bemoan the absence of God's speech, who cry out for personal communication with God Himself. They want cues for their lines. They want explanations and specific directions from the Artist.

And God, as far as they can tell, is ignoring them. They feel neglected—because they weren't cast as Moses or Elijah or Enoch or Gideon.

Tell me what you want me to do, God. Speak to me (in English, please) and tell me if I should take this job in Des Moines or stay closer to my mother.

Then, because their part in this story does not include cosmic voice-overs in English, they enter into an existential crisis. They begin to "doubt."

What kind of story do you think this is? I have no problem with the pettiness of your Des Moines dilemma. The world spins on through space, bowled by its Maker. The sun burns on, hot with His words, and yet He still crafts every snowflake without digital shortcuts. He knows that you want to move to Des Moines and yet you feel guilty. He wrote the story. He crafted your character. He gave you life and a plot of your own. Even simple character stories, the kind with no special effects, put together by one lonely producer and starring unbeautiful people, even those are not beneath Him. Infinite reaches all the way up into the transcendent epics of the stars, and all the way down into the ant hill where one loyal worker spends his life toiling, from its first day after the larval stage to its noble end, killed by a ladybug while defending the colony's vulnerable herd of aphids.

The ant's story may be more dramatic than yours, but it's not bigger. And don't worry, some day you'll play for keeps too. Some day, even in slow, suburban stories, there will come a death scene.

But why would any Christian claim that God has stopped talking? Did He speak the world into existence? Does matter exist apart from Him? Is it still here? Are you still here? Then He is still speaking.

Step outside your front door and look at today's stage. Speak. God will reply. He will speak to you. He gave you senses. Use them. He will parade His art. He will give you a scene, a setting for the day. He will give you conflict to overcome, opportunities for your character to grow or fail.

But do not expect Him to speak in English. And do not expect Him to stay on whatever topic you might choose. His attention is everywhere and no story should be easy, as every reader knows.

You are on your porch. Look at the blue sky.

God, am I going to get this sale today? The commission would pay for a boat.

Look at this squirrel, He says. Do you understand it? Do you know what it means? What does it tell you about me? Watch its tail snap. You're the only one watching. You and I are alone in the audience, sharing this scene. What does it remind you of?

I need this sale.

There's an ant on your shoe. It's a good ant. Last spring it turned the tide in the great Sidewalk Crack War of D Street. One of its grandfathers traveled half a mile with Lewis and Clark. Did you know that today it dies? That you are its death?

I wish I had a new car. Hyundais are lame.

In the time of Noah, there was a small creature, tinier than could be seen. After a long journey and many struggles, today its descendant will be at your office. Even now, it is barely clinging to life on a microwave button, desperate to reproduce before the end. The drama is incredible, actually. The narrative is intricate. You wouldn't believe all the twists and reversals it took to get it there.

Why do I have to work with Roger on this one? Roger's two tons of no fun.

The creature will live. Tomorrow you will have pink eye.

I could never believe in a God that makes eyes itch. And the tear duct goop is an added insult.

The apostle Paul: God made your eyes. Can He not make them pink?

What about Des Moines? How does a squirrel, an ant, a single ambassador of conjunctivitis help *me* with *my* problem?

Who are you? What kind of novel are you in? What is the conflict? If you were reading this story, watching an omniscient (really) narrator describe you, your innermost thoughts, your insecurities, and all your desires, would you have any trouble at all giving your character counsel? Would it be oh-so-difficult to tell when that character was motivated from selfishness or pride? Would you love to see that story written? Would you like to see yourself as you are, as you *really* are, with not one of your thoughts or impulses omitted?

Maybe you're not a lecherous youth pastor, a hypocritical abstinence counselor, or a thieving neighbor. But you are something. A backstabbing friend? An insecure bully of a father? An unfaithful husband? A resentful wife? What? Trot out your thoughts, every last one, no matter how tiny, no matter how fleeting, no matter how awful or pornographic. Project them on a screen for the viewing public. We'd have you pegged in a heartbeat—just as you'd be able to peg us. A good author could even work with the unhidden things, the things you're actually willing for the rest of us to see. Are you a whining fusser? Do you complain about the weather? Do you know how much work went into that weather system? Maybe you resent any obstacle, anything that makes your day longer or harder. You think you're underappreciated. You, with the way you think about everyone else around you (your mother, your siblings, coworkers, or even your spouse), feel undervalued. What exactly is your value? Would the planet miss you if you ceased to be? Would the human race falter?

We are always on stage. We are always in a novel, and even when no other characters are around, the art continues. The Triune audience watches. You have been given your body. You have been given your ancestors, your natural strengths and your natural weaknesses. The backstory is all in place. You have been drawn, described, and placed on a stage unlike any other—the Globe. And you have been given your freedom to act. Your story has begun already. It began when that lucky, eager sperm stood on the winner's platform and listened to its national anthem.

One tail flick slower and you would be someone else. You would be named Theresa now and you wouldn't be you. Theresa would have been better at this whole life thing. Would have been more beautiful. Good at the piano. Loved by all who knew her.

Or not. Apparently you were worth bringing onto this stage. But why? Are you here as an extra in somebody else's scene? Are you here as a casualty? A comic throwaway? The girl who drops her top and starts the horror film? Are you here to fall in love by chance, be given a beautiful life, and then burn it all to hell in five short minutes at a Motel 6? Are you a cautionary tale?

We are all watching. We are all watched.

To some people, this could seem glamorous. The whole idea of being in a novel or film or reality show is quite appealing.

We know what kind of people they are. We can see the shallowness, the superficiality of their self-love. But for some reason, they can't. For some reason, none of us can when we are set on making asses of ourselves. Listen to your dialogue. Look at your thoughts. Be horrified. Be grateful that God loves characters, and loves characters on journeys, characters honestly striving to grow. If someone else was delivering your lines, would you like them? If someone else was wearing your attitude, would you be impressed?

I love the story. I love being in the story because there are beetles and my wife and my children with wide eyes and ticklish ribs and dirt that smells and hands that blister and wasps and moths and every-flavored wind. I love seeing the story because it shows me who I am and how far I need to go. Because it knocks me down and waits to see if I'll get up. Because we are always standing on a cliff's edge, and the danger is real. The choices in front of you never go away. Scene after scene is given to you and the teeming universe in the audience waits for your reaction, for your line, waits to see if you'll yell at the fat-faced child who spilled the milk, or if you'll laugh and kiss a cheek. What kind of father will you be in *their* story? The hump on their back that will always haunt them, the one who gave them damage to overcome? The one who's too busy? The one who drinks? The one who cheats?

Walk the cliff. Watch yourself walk the cliff. The ocean is always there, devouring.

What will your character do when the petty things happen, when your car betrays you in the cold? When the pipes freeze? When God knowingly places ice on the sidewalk beneath your feet? When the sun sets beautifully while you needle your wife? Do you laugh at the jokes and love the lovely? Are you too important to be amused at your own finitude? Are you unaware that your bowels move daily? How lofty are you?

A friend once told me how he lost his fingertips. He crafted his story with care. He nursed it—bloody sawdust, shocked deafness, early dialogue. He pitched himself as an antihero, complete with delirium, hilarity while on the anesthetic, and an attraction to his nurse.

I laughed. He laughed. He meant me to. Another listening friend, a girl, snapped at us.

"Why would you laugh?" she asked. "That's awful."

My friend and I looked at each other.

"Because it's funny," I said.

He snorted and held up his hand. "It was just my fingers."

My brother-in-law lost fingertips in a lawn mower. They were reattached. At least until he slammed one in a car door and it came off. He threw it in the trash. There were places to go.

◆

On the jetty, I turn for a final look. The storm is filling the harbor with sand. Rain drips off my hood and runs down my nose. My legs chafe as they shift inside wet denim.

The ocean sprawls. At the horizon, the gray sky meets with the gray sea and the two become one, a seamless wall of storm. Closer, spray rises behind the lighthouse.

"Cold," I say.

Cold, God says. And wet.

The rhythms are rough. I am part of a line, one word in a collection chosen for this day, this scene. His salty syllables sting my cheeks, and He continues to speak—

The beaches must be tilled, He says. The kelp beds have grown too thick. The cliffs need new holes. The cliff-dwelling rich need new leaks. The seas have been asking to toss. The sharks need to feel small. The seals and dolphins are laughing. They always are. You could learn from them.

"Cold," my wife says. And we turn.

TALKING ROCKS

This morning I spat on a tree. I hope it didn't mind. I intended to clock how long it took for my spittle to freeze. But I got distracted buckling my son in the car. By the time I was done and checked back, the molecular structure had expanded and the tree had a little bit of extra shine, a little twinkle in its trunk. My art. My personal expression.

Under two minutes.

Nutshell art theory distilled from Tolstoy (and others): Art is the communication of an experience or sensation, real or imagined.

Cold is a sensation. Has it been communicated?

This cold wave has pleased me. The cold is of the sort that the wise men, the priests and weather-watchers, refer to as zero.

I don't know what a degree is, but thirty-two or fewer are necessary for ice-making. Today those degrees are all missing. They've taken a day off, collectively staying home in sweatpants. I can't blame them. The rearview mirror usually counts them for me. Zero.

When they're not around, things get brisk.

My son is waiting in his seat, but there's something I must do first. Something I have waited for. I inhale strongly through my nose and feel the pinch as ice crystals form inside my nostrils, tugging discreetly at the hairs. I inhale harder, sucking my nostrils tight against the central structure of my nose. It has happened. I stop breathing. My nostrils have frozen shut.

I walk around the car savoring the sensation. If someone offered to pinch my nose, the mailman, for example, I would decline, more or less politely. But when the world does it, when an intangible but chilly cosmic hand makes the offer, I cannot refuse.

To exist in this poem is a greater gift than any finite creature can imagine. To be so insignificant and yet still be given a speaking part, to be given scenes that are my own, and my own only, scenes where the audience is limited to the Author Himself (scenes that I often flub), to have been here with my frozen nose, to have been crafted with at least as much care as a snowflake (though I'm harder to melt), and to hear and feel and see and taste and smell the heavy poetry of God, that is enough.

Exhaling, I feel the thaw. I should be in the car driving. We're late, and kindergarten waits for no man.

◆

It is strange to me that in the cold moments, with my chapped cheeks and cold-dried teeth, I am closer to the sun than I will be in the August heat. It's all about refraction and reflection. Where I sit now, high up on my native planet, I am tipping away from the sun. The distance between us is smaller, but we're having trouble communicating. The pesky atmosphere is garnering a slice of solar love for itself, and the reduction in energy is just enough to make snowflakes possible.

I have tried to ponder the bizarreness of our exact position in space. If I were able to run probabilities of this nature (if anyone were able to run probabilities of this nature), then I would like to know what the chances are of a huge sphere ending up spinning around a much huger burning sphere (without plummeting in . . . yet), set at exactly the right distance away, such that temperatures are cool enough that we don't all shrivel up like wrist hairs too close to a barbecue, and warm enough that we don't all end up like the mammoths surprised by fast-growing glaciers. (Imagine a glacier fast enough to sneak up on you and surround you in ice while you innocently munched on a buttercup.) Even less likely, the axis of our bowling-ball-home is tipping just so, angling us enough that on one side of our annual lap (at least where I live), we are toasty and light fireworks, and on the other, we jingle bells and heat up chocolate. What are the odds? Anyone? Would any Las Vegas bookie be willing to give me numbers on the chance of it happening again?

Probabilities. They are the prophets of a mechanical god.

Assume that the ultimate overseer of this reality is someone named Chance (with highlighted hair and poor management skills), and assume that everything in existence happens randomly (thanks to him), without any consideration for the artistry of it. Let us explore the general unlikelihood of anything ever happening, ever.

Rumor has it that most normal men send at least eight million "forward swimming" sperm looking for an egg every sexual act. Don't even bother adding in egg variation, or the total number of sperm that may have had a fighting chance during your mother's days of fertility when you were conceived (or the possibility that she might have taken her friends' advice and shunned your father). Keep it simple and wildly conservative. Your chances of being here were about one out of eight million. Funny. Those were my odds too. The chances of us both being here? One out of sixty-four trillion. The chances of us both being on the same round planet, leaning far enough away from the sun that our nostrils freeze shut but we don't die? The chances of us both being on the same round planet buzzing around the same star, with six billion other very particular people all simultaneously in existence? It makes me tired, like the cold. And I don't know what numbers bigger than a googolplex are called, especially since a googol is supposed to be bigger than the number of elementary particles in the "observable universe" (whatever that means), and a googolplex is a one with that many zeros after it. I've been told that the whole concept was invented by a nine-year-old named Milton.

But I'm not letting it rest. Not yet. One more round of odds.

Start with your grandparents. What were the odds of all four of them blinking, crying, and discovering that they existed? Assuming that surviving, finding each other, and getting married was a sure thing (and keeping the variables limited to a single procreative act), what were the odds of both your parents being conceived? Assuming that finding each other and getting to work on you was also a sure thing, what were the odds that you would be the result?

One out of 2.097152 ... wait ... I think I just screwed that up. Duodecillion? No. That only has thirty-nine zeros. Should we just go with umpteen? You get the point, don't you? You basically have no chance of being here and you should quit trying already. Getting your hopes up will only make it hurt more when you don't happen.

We are a world of lottery winners. For every one of us here right now, in every begetting, there were at least 7,999,999 losers. They don't even know how almost they were.

"I wish I'd never been born," the adolescent moans.

"Shut up, Randy. There are eight million other kids who would be wishing they could be here right now if only they were here to wish."

What are the odds that something painted by Rembrandt will be beautiful, potent, and worth hanging on your wall? It's a sure thing. Bet on it. Chance has nothing to do with Rembrandt. Chance has nothing to do with anything as far as I can tell, thank God. If he did, this world would look worse than a canvas by Jackson Pollock.

This air I'm breathing that thaws out my nostrils, where was it a week ago? Where was it a year ago? These molecules of carbon and oxygen that I steam into the cosmos, where were they while Rome was burning? What tree, what fish, what strange or awfully normal creature used this carbon in its flesh, pumped this oxygen in its blood? Am I breathing parts of Genghis Khan's horse? No doubt this carbon started long ago, in a distant thistle or bit of bark. How many times has it been consumed, expelled, and consumed again? How many reincarnations has it seen, or am I working with virgin air? I doubt it. Breathing where no man has breathed before is harder than it sounds.

There are times when staring at the stars that I suddenly shiver and feel a sort of cosmic dizziness, times when my mind zooms out, and I am looking down at myself standing on this bizarre marble, times when I can see the heavenly hordes, stars crowded beneath and above, when the world actually feels as big and wild as it is. The world can make me motion sick. It can make me laugh nervously until my jaw aches. Am I old enough to be on this ride? When was its last inspection? I can't find my seat belt, and I can hear someone screaming to get off.

But it's not always the stars, not always the massive expanses of the heavenlies, that make my knees wobble.

There was a day years ago, a day between the winter and spring, when the sun was beginning to flex and find its way through our angled atmosphere and the ice was becoming living water, dripping off of needled trees. I sat shivering on a log that had fallen across a stream, watching the water rush beneath me with its rounded back. Small wooded hills surrounded us. It was there, listening to the hum of liquid hurry, that I first began to feel these thoughts, when I began to feel like a word among words, understanding the divine language of creation but unable to speak it myself.

I knew what God was saying. He gave me eyes so that I might see Him say it. He gave me ears so I could pick up the rhythms and clatters and rhymes. My skin can tighten, teased by His breath, and send up bumps. My tongue can taste these words, the water, the pine needles, even the log that held me, but I cannot say them. We have given them names, shortcutting them with smaller sounds, sounds that fit in our mouths.

Tree, I say, and you know what I mean. You see one in your mind, or glance out your window and remember the much-needed pruning. Tree, God says, and there is one. But He doesn't say the word *tree*; He says the tree itself. He needs no shortcut. He's not merely calling one into existence, though His voice creates. His voice *is* its existence. That thing in your yard, that mangy apple or towering spruce, that thing is not the referent of His word. It is His word and its referent. If He were to stop talking, it wouldn't be there. Or do you think that its molecules and atoms and quarks are made of some mysterious, self-sustaining matter that has always been and will always be, some infinite Play-Doh or hydrogen, holy be its name? Maybe there was an Adam Up Quark and an Eve Lepton? Maybe God found a bit of infinite matter and blew it up like a balloon, and now it sputters and spits while it swirls, sustaining itself? Maybe the balloon found itself and did its own huffing and puffing. Place your faith in the infinitude of matter if you like, and Chance will write the story. He'll shuffle together pages, words, scribbles from different languages, other people's noses, and small bits of string, run it all through a mulcher, and spray it into your yard. Enjoy your novel.

Imagine a poem written with such enormous three-dimensional words that we had to invent a smaller word to reference each of the big ones; that we had to rewrite the whole thing in shorthand, smashing it into two dimensions, just to talk about it. Or don't imagine it. Look outside. Human language is our attempt at navigating God's language; it is us running between the lines of His epic, climbing on the vowels and building houses out of the consonants.

See that thing?

What thing?

That huge pile of stone that climbs to where the air gets thin?

Yes. It has a lot of syllables.

Let's call it a mountain, okay? When I say mountain, that's what I mean. It'll be easier than building one every time.

Is it supposed to blow up?

Let's call it a volcano.

We feel the need to communicate with each other about this thing we're on, this spinning thing we can't get off. We combine language and imagination and do our best. But our words fall short. They're just noises in the air and flat ink on a page. And so we paint. We poke clay. We develop theories of architecture. We write poems and novels and produce grainy independent films. All to communicate . . . how the world makes us feel? To make others feel the same? To proselytize? To remind others of what we all know, of what we all see, of what we all have felt, and then make them go through it again?

We imitate God's words, but our noises are insufficient. So we doodle in the margins, children working to capture the Sistine Chapel with finger paints on a paper plate. What else can we do?

My father uses a blue highlighter to remind him of the good bits he reads, but it has trouble sticking to sunsets or thunderstorms or the cries of the meadowlark in the Spring. His guitar is more helpful.

A thought from C. S. Lewis, boiled down and removed from its original habitat: Art has no survival value, but gives survival value.

On that day, sitting on my log in the early stirrings of spring, the stream overwhelmed me. I sat, staring, trying to comprehend its sheer massiveness. Yes, its massiveness. I could have jumped over it (maybe) and yet it was beyond comprehension. I wanted to know how many molecules were sliding past me per minute. I wanted to know where they had spent their lives, lives that stretched back to the beginning of the world. Most of them had probably been snow, recently delicate, now reveling in the rough and tumble world of a fast mountain stream. Before the snow, where had they been? Steam coming off a cow's back? Evaporation from a kiddie pool? Most were probably oceanic. Formerly waves. But before then? How many times had each of these molecules fallen from the sky, contributing some little corner to a snowflake? How many times divorced into lonely hydrogen and oxygen, how many times remarried? These things had traveled, no doubt. These things had even been around when Moses did his business with the Red Sea. Had they been there? Had they heard about it from friends?

There is water somewhere in the world that ran down the body of the Word Himself as John, His cousin, baptized Him. No doubt it is water still, uncherished by man, known only by the Author of this story. Drops were chosen to serve as His tears beside Jerusalem, more were chosen to wait in His side for the tip of a Roman spear. They burst forth and completed their poetic calling, a flourish in the story, a picture within a picture.

But did that water retire? Does it no longer have a task? Has God made sure it never entered a toilet tank or moistened the parched lips of a liar? Why would He? He has never treated Himself as sacred. That's our role. We are the ones who scurry over relics and conjure up more when they're difficult to find. Put me back on my log, back in that lost moment, swallowed by forgotten sensation. Is some of the Red Sea flowing beneath me while I shiver on my perch? Are the tears of Christ, the waters from His side, now mingling with cattle urine and melting snow and pillars of rank steam chuffed from industrial chimneys? Are the whales spouting sacred drops off the coast of Oregon? Or are those drops washing the hands of a murderer?

Does God shape each water molecule with the care He puts into His snowflakes? He needs no shortcuts to name them, no broad categories. He knows them each, every last one. He knows where they have been and where they are going. He knows their uniqueness and which of the holiest ancient drops are now in relationships that would appall any human sensibilities. If I could know the complete history of one cubic foot of this stream, then I could know the history of the world.

As for God, His Son turned water into wine. And so we end the story before He turned that wine into urine. (Should we deny that He did?)

I spat on a tree in the frigid cold. But what was that spit really? Where will it be when I have turned to leather inside my box?

I wish these things could talk to me, logs, streams, and all of their parts. But they *are* all talking to me. It takes all five of my senses and mental extrapolation, imagination, just to hear the things around me in the moment. They don't speak my short-hand, they don't know my compressed and lifeless, two-dimensional language. My tongue can make an *L* sound, but it can't quite make a log. Write me a history of every existing thing flattened onto pages. Crowd it into English. One novel, one volume per thing, one page per year. That should be enough abridgement. I'll check them all out from the library and pore over every page—I swear I will. The story of a driveway rock in six thousand pages. A different six-thousand-page story for *every* driveway rock—volcanoes, floods, crushers, asphalt crews. You don't buy into such a young earth? Fine. Add the extra pages. I'll read them too.

The infinite Creator has an infinite attention span, an infinite love of detail. In His story, every prop must have a complete history. Every extra must have a complete genealogy. And the set must be convincing. Spare no expense. There should be three-dimensional graphics, convincing sound-effects, and something to break up the background blackness of the night sky, something tasteful like a few billion solar systems flaming and spurting, spitting colored worlds and sparking stars, set far enough away to achieve an understated twinkle (like my spit on the tree). Real stars are illegal in most states. You have to get them on the reservation.

I've watched scientists try to explain what it would be like to encounter a creature from the fourth dimension (you know, the fourth one). They are all in agreement. We wouldn't even know that it was four-dimensional. We would simply sense it and interact with it in terms of our own three dimensions, the same way a blind man interprets the world in terms of his four remaining senses.

We are all blind. How many senses are possible that are not included within our natures? What's the fully loaded model like? How could we know? We are all limited to five senses (that we're sure of), and we must live in and interact with this world, with art and language that is much too big for us. But we also have our imaginations and a creative impulse of our own. We watch, we study, we try to translate and understand the enormity of the story going on around us. We try to process a play that has been written *by* the infinite *for* the infinite. We are overwhelmed. We feel this story in any number of ways beyond the mere sum of our physical senses. We empathize and sympathize. We grieve. Our bodies shake and our eyes spring water when someone is taken away, when another character, one that we loved and knew, disappears from our range of sensation. We laugh.

When things surprise and please us with their twists and turns, our lips peel up and we show our teeth. Some people lose their eyes inside the skin of their face, and all of us experience spasms in the gut, a diaphragm momentarily unhinged, imitating the unpredictability of what we've seen.

We have been given many tools to get at this world, to become members of the audience as well as players on the stage. We can step off the canvas (if only slightly) and examine a part of the painting. We are trapped within the art, but the art is so profound that we are self-aware. We are unable to focus on the story of every rock, unable to find out what every molecule in every snowflake really looks like, unable to watch the great race of our own conception.

But do we *need* to see it all? Look around you. Sense around you. What is being said; what flavor is the story that swirls in your immediate paragraph and which character are you within it? Are you even narrower than you have to be? Are you ungrateful? Do you find just one element of the story, one note from the song, and then dwell there? Squirrels are run over in this world. People, young and old, die and exit the stage. Is that all you see? Then choose your music accordingly. Get some black eyeliner and stay home from work.

When you look at the stars do you despair at your own smallness? Are you unable to be just one snowflake in the blizzard of this reality? Are you afraid of open spaces? Of the bigness of God, of the crashing ocean and the fact that at some point your time here will end? Or does your own smallness make you laugh?

There is a crushing joy that crackles in every corner of this world. I am tiny and yet I am here. I have been given senses, awareness, existence, and placed on a stage so crowded with the vast, so teeming with the tiny, that I can do nothing but laugh, and sometimes laugh and cry.

Living makes dying worth it.

Ayn Rand (patronizingly simplified): Art concretizes man's metaphysical abstractions, relaying to him what is important about his own existence.

Is that all?

It is hard to stay focused with so much swirling around me. God is distracting. He never stops talking, and I can never stop listening.

There is a reason we sleep.

There is a butterfly (my children and I have only ever watched it on film) that does not worry about its young. It lays an egg on a leaf and flies away. The egg hatches and the unworried larva rolls onto the ground.

It will die. It has no way to feed itself, no way to know what the world is or where we are going or even that life and death are different from each other. But it is not worried. There are ants in this world.

Ants collect the larva and take it into their nests, down through tunnels, storing it with their own young in the nursery chambers. It is bigger than the ant young, and it is pink. But they do not care. They keep it clean and fed.

Scientists say that the ants cannot tell the difference. Maybe they can't. Maybe they can. It is enough for them that the orphan exists untended. Its size and its color and its species are unimportant. We dismiss their good deed and point to their ignorance. Perhaps their ignorance is the good deed.

At the very least, there is a wasp who can tell the difference between the adopted and biological young. From the air, it locates the ant nests that have taken in these foster children. It invades. Drugging the ants into confusion, the wasp hurries down through the tunnels, hunting for what it already knows is there. In the nursery chamber the wasp ignores the larval ants. It seeks the pink, and when one is found, the wasp mounts it, arching its back and driving its abdomen down, impaling the well-cleaned, well-fed butterfly infant. A single egg is laid inside the larva, and the wasp moves on, searching for others, piercing as many as it can before the confused ants find their minds.

Each larva hardens, pupating, turning to soup within stiff walls. The soup reforms. While ants watch, two creatures are born. From each unpierced there comes a butterfly. With soft blue wings dragging behind it, the insect makes its way above ground. The beautiful wings spread and stiffen in the sun. The ants watch. It is a child to be proud of.

Another pupa has burst as well, and a wasp hurries to the surface.

Wasps are villains in many stories.

As for the mayfly, it spends its life underwater. It has a cycle not uncommon in the insect world, complicated and difficult. It is not the path of least resistance. It is not an arc tailored by nature for any advantage in reproduction. No pragmatic god designed this.

For two years the mayfly swims beneath the surface. When finally it climbs into the air, the fish and birds salivate. The surviving males molt and molt until they reach adulthood.

Adulthood will last for thirty minutes. The male has no stomach and no mouth. He has only a small store of larval energy and nothing to lose.

The bacchic frenzy begins. Half an hour. Half an hour to fly and fight and mate. Half an hour to avoid the jumping fish and diving birds and batter down female resistance.

Please, I only have thirty minutes to live.

It might work in the human world, but mayflies have it rough.

Cry me a river. You and every other guy I know.

She might be willing. She might not. One way or another, you'll be dead by lunch.

G. K. Chesterton (from the *Illustrated London News*, no less): "Art, like morality, consists of drawing the line somewhere."

What is art?

You are. And the mayfly. And every wasp novel ever lived. And the hard Winter overthrown by Spring. Motherhood. Grass. Jupiter. Your annoying neighbor.

Art is.

◆

The sun is warming now, or the atmosphere is tired of fighting.

Rivulets are forming in the street. The degrees are back. Ice never wins.

Good-bye, I say to the snowflakes. You lived longer than the mayflies.

Don't worry about it, they say. We're going to a better place. Where?

The ocean mostly. Some of us will walk, some will fly. Some of us are actually booked for Asia. No offense, but we're ready to move on. Not a lot going on here apart from the dog.

Sorry about the yellow. It's not my dog.

The jaundiced flakes laugh. We don't mind. That dog-water has really lived. Great stories. It was an honor.

◆

Do you understand photosynthesis? Especially the whole making-trees-and-leaves-and-fruit-out-of-thin-air part? Go blow on that bush. You can't see it, but the bush will turn your breath into raspberry juice. We could improve on the name. *Photosynthesis*. I've suggested Green Magyk, but no one listens to me.

The grass is reappearing, brown and tired, packed into turf graves. But the sun will bring it back. I've read this story before, but I don't think I can spoil it by giving away the end. It all comes back to life and it will get so thick I'll actually have to cut it down. Repeatedly. We've invented special machines.

This air is cool, but it feels warm because it's not biting me. Spring is not here, but the promise of spring is. I feel like an Old Testament hermit, a prophet waiting for the world to thaw, waiting for the days to get longer and the sun to shine brighter, waiting for a dead world to come back to life.

The crocuses will be first, over on the south side of the house. Spring is worth the wait. Life is worth the death.

I walk down to the gray stone wall by the street. Some dog has dropped a winter gift by my car door. I will not think about what that matter once was, or all the amazing things that it might still become. I think about what it is right now, in this line of the story. And in this line of the story, I have a job to do.

When it's done, I lean against the stones and look around at the gray melting world, at the tree trunk now without my twinkle.

I like my basalt wall. It grows moss well, and it's a good home for the five-inch slugs that will leave shine trails on the sidewalk in the summer.

These rocks blew up once. At some point they were liquid, vomited up by a planet.

I slap one.

It says nothing, but it means something. All words do. At the least, it means itself, a retaining wall for me and a home for the slugs.

I like words I can slap.

WINTER HIATUS: BREAKING TEETH

I see my grandfather walking between shoveled mounds of snow, moving slowly beneath the load of life. He is a block away from where I stand at an office window, and still I can see his lips moving, unable to swallow back the hymns and prayers within him. This is my ancestor, father to my father, an old jug, cracked and spilling warmth along his path.

Wipe two decades off my age. Put me in pajamas and place me at another window, a window in my grandparents' aging, sagging, cracking, yellow house. It is New Year's Eve, my parents' anniversary. Outside the world is cold, and the night has most likely passed its middle, easing into the first dark moments of a young year. But in the winter, midnight darkness takes a different flavor.

Deep, white, shimmering swarms of crystals are mounded on the hills and piled perfectly on every tree branch. I stand, shivering, looking out the window at a pearl-world beaming beneath the face of a moon as bright as it is silent. A forest of thick icicles stretches down past the side windows, bending and muddying the moonlight.

My grandparents are long asleep, but my two sisters watch me, bundled in their sleeping bags beside popping embers in the living room fireplace, protected from the sparks by a tired wire screen.

My grandfather is like his house. Once strong and young, now his beams and timbers sag beneath the weight of long use, heavier even than the piles of snow on his roof and the fanged ice stretching down from the gutters. The Nebraska farm boy rowed for Navy. He served well in Korea. He turned a sharp mind and a bulldog jaw to a lifetime of chasing souls. Though many of his victims now carry on his work, he will not stop until his roof collapses beneath the winter.

At the window, back in my youth, I shiver again. My skin rises up in mountain ranges, but I savor the cold. This cold, this bite, and the draft I can feel ghosting through the old glass panes are all preparing me for the beautiful sleeve of warmth that is my sleeping bag. The fire pops, tempting me, but still I stand, staring at the creeping cold, marveling at the icicles. In this house, they are the winter's front lines—a Berlin Wall raised up (or down) between hibernating life and the killing cold. This house is like its occupants. It has never held its heat selfishly. Heat is its gift to the world, and the icicles form in retaliation. Yearly, on this one winter night, when our parents leave, my grandfather stokes a fire, blocks it with a screen, and throws our bags on the floor beside it. Sometimes he tips the couches onto their faces and shoves them together as a fort. Always, we are allowed to burn inappropriate things in the fire—trash mostly—and the strange dancing colors entertain while we lie on the floor, whispering.

The moon peers through tree branches, and the knobbed icicle shafts snare its light. These are icicles that threaten to reach the ground, winter fangs gnawing at the house, straining the eaves.

I move to the door and slip thin feet into oversized boots. I will not need a coat. I am cold already.

My older sister sits up. The door opens and the winter lunges in, snapping cold at my shins and arms and face, rolling invisibly across the floor to the sleeping bags.

I am outside, the door is closed, and my skin is the color of moonlight.

I cannot shiver. My joints are hardening. Lunging off the sidewalk, I hurry toward the corner of the house, toward the greatest of the ice teeth. Snow avalanches into my boots. Needles of air, thorns of cold dig into me as I grab at the biggest icicle. A third comes away in my hands. The rest drops to the ice carnage in the drift below. Picking up a chunk, I hurl it at the remaining row of gaping teeth. A jaw breaks. Fangs tumble.

Turning, quaking, I run back to the house, back to the heat.

Flippancy toward winter, petty sneers and disrespect for the cold were important for us in those days. Cold could not be our master.

My children have a name for my grandmother. She is Chi-Chi-Pa. They named her for the Japanese song she sings, a relic of her missionary days, a time when she could walk without struggling and pain was not such a part of her existence. She smiles and laughs when my children steal her walker, when Spring borrows a prop from Winter.

As far back as I have memory, she has had her own funeral hymns chosen. She has love and warmth and joy, but she can't help but anticipate the end. She is eager for the ice to fall away from her joints, for her eyes to burn bright. She has labored long. She has sons and a daughter who love and honor her. She has seen the rich harvest of fifteen grandchildren and already thirteen great-grandchildren. She is happy, but she is eager.

When the final collapse comes, when the ice triumphs, she at least will have no truck with grief. Let the Winter come. It is the only path to Spring. The house is battered with cold, but inside there is a warmth that cannot and will not die.

Both of my sisters are up, talking, whispering to me and laughing quietly as I shut the door and kick off my boots, as the icicle shard drips in my hands.

Inset into the old fireplace, there is a strange little stove with open iron doors and a smooth iron cap. The dripping icicle goes onto the cap, and we three huddle to watch. The winter fang spins and sizzles and twists in pain while it shrinks, leaving a dark, fast-vanishing trail.

We watch until not a trace remains, until the winter's bite has taken invisibly to the air. Then, triumphant, we shovel ourselves back into bags and stare at the fire, sure that we will not sleep before the embers do, unafraid of the winter, lulled into comfort by the warmth, lulled into sleep by its whispers.

UNWOMB THE WORLD

Spring—look to the sun.

I'm eating my lunch in a graveyard. Human seeds have been planted in neat little rows. Stone stakes label the crop.

My back is against a wall, and while I chew, my eyes wander.

Not ten feet from me, a Richard has been planted. He was planted three decades ago. There is a space on the stone for another name, room in the ground for another seed, the completion of a pair.

The sun is bright, but doing less than I had hoped it would. The ground is wet and cold. I'm in Maryland, lingering behind an old gray church. The Spring is struggling, young.

The sun livens the ground where it falls, but only briefly. Clouds, damnable clouds, interfere with its grace.

It doesn't matter. These seeds need more than the sun can give.

I stand and move through the rows, reading labels and predictions. Some time and effort has been put into these markers, money spent so we won't forget where to water and weed and watch, so we won't forget where we put that other pea from our pod.

There is a small stone that catches my eye, framed for one moment in gold laughter too fast for the clouds to hold back. The light passes, but the stone remains, on the far side of the churchyard, threatened from behind by an overgrown hedgerow.

Water seeps up around my shoes while I walk, and I can't help but think how cold these beds must be. But moisture is good for a garden.

I remember the sun and the clouds and the cold on that day seven years ago. I remember the hedge crowding around the little stone. I remember standing and staring, crouching down, reading the name and resolving never to forget.

But I have forgotten. Alice? Margaret?

I know only that the girl had been in the ground for fifty years, that she'd been two when her hole had been dug, and that fresh flowers tied with string lay on her grave.

Someone needed no stone reminder, and a fifty-year-old separation was as fresh as those flowers. For me, even that stone was not enough. We shall all be forgotten in the end. Deaths are as common as births. More common.

In Cape Cod, my wife and I watched tight little grave gardens move past our windows while we traveled toward the sea.

The stones are thin and worn smooth, cut and carved too

shallow for long remembering. Here there are seeds in the ground planted at random, with stakes confused or bleached blank. What will grow? We can only watch and wait for the spring. Tomatoes, maybe. Zucchini. But this is Cape Cod. There will be a heavy crop of sailors. How many of these stones actually mark a burial place? How many have been set up in memoriam, holding only a name in remembrance, a name that was swallowed by the sea? A name forgotten even by the stone.

In the rest of the country, we plant our dead. We work them into the soil, the same soil that gives us our food. Through the history of the cape, many thousands have been planted in the sea. Their names were carved in stone and in the souls of those who loved them. Their bodies fattened the lobster crop.

Look out at the world. See death and pain, injustice and grief. How could this be a poem if God is the Poet?

Evil, the problem of.

If God is both all powerful and all good, then how can there be evil in the world?

Option One (of three, according to David Hume, the skeptical Scotsman): God is all powerful but not all good. Evil is dandy fine with Him.

Option Two: God is all good but not all powerful. He sees all the evil in the world, but He is impotent when it comes to doing anything about it. If it is any consolation, He would do something if He could. At least we think so.

Option Three: There is no God. Welcome to the meatgrinder of Chance.

Place your bets. Place your lives.

Gottfried Leibniz (picture a math brain plus a rational, optimistic philosophy plus an enormous eighteenth-century wig) has most likely provoked more usages of this argument than any other thinker. He pushed the attributes of God in the opposite direction. If (he began) God is all good, all powerful, and in every way perfect, then this must be the best of all possible worlds, a world not to be improved upon. Surely, an omniperfect God could create no less.

And of course, Leibniz's reasoning appears to be sound (given his axioms). But that hasn't prevented him from being mocked—in his own time, and in every philosophy department down to the present.

For that, I admire him.

In *For the Time Being*, Annie Dillard attempts to keep God around and keep Him nice (if weepy). And so she (like many others) scraps omnipotence. "The very least likely things for which God might be responsible are what insurers call 'acts of God.'"

Go that route. Katrina wasn't Him. Nothing involving fault lines is Him. Stop looking at Him like that—He's never so much as touched a tornado. He exists, and He's friendly, but if you're in some kind of trouble, you might just want to make a deal with the devil. Go to the man in charge, I always say. You can renege later, and you might get really good at the guitar in the meantime.

◆

Croesus was no intellectual beacon (despite the fact that he invented money). He was the king of Lydia, and when one of his concubines gave birth to a lion cub, he naturally consulted an oracle.

"Carry the cub around the walls of your city, and it shall become invincible," she said, speaking on behalf of Apollo.

Croesus carried it most of the way around the city walls but skipped the bit on top of a cliff. Nobody could ever climb that part.

Any kid could tell you what happens next, but apparently Croesus didn't read the right stories when he was young. When a god gives you advice, you'd better avert your eyes, keep your head down, and make damn sure you follow it to the letter. If you don't, that god will come for your scalp.

Unless you know a bigger god, or better yet, are related to one by blood.

Armies came, climbed the cliff, and Croesus, the most powerful man then percolating on that part of the planet, rejoined the great circle of life.

Agamemnon's fleet got marooned on an island on its way to rid the world of Trojans—the ships were dead in a windless sea.

The poor guy had to sacrifice his own daughter just to get the wind he needed from the gods. To make things worse, after a decade-plus of ravaging the coast of Asia Minor, just doing his best to support the family, he gets home and his irritated (now daughterless) wife murders him in his bath.

Honestly, was it his fault?

We could talk about Oedipus, the poor, accidentally incestuous and patricidal king. Fate worked him over at record levels.

Odysseus had better luck. Various beings with control over "acts of God" managed to get everyone around him eaten, drowned, addicted to the lotus flower, and turned into pigs. Neptune wanted him dead because he'd blinded the Cyclops (rather than allowing himself to be eaten), and Apollo finished off the last of his friends after they ate some of his sacred cows. Odysseus was even kept as a nymph's somewhat discontent (he did cry on the beach at night) sex slave for seven years. But in the end, he managed to get strings pulled. Zeus and Athena got him home, enabling him to slaughter all the trespassers who had been pursuing his "widow."

As far as the Greek heroes were concerned, Odysseus had himself a couple happy decades.

The ancient Greeks had a theory: The world (and everyone in it) is out to screw you. Screw it (and them) first. Do your best to appease the most powerful gods, but in the end it won't matter. You'll be mulched. If you're lucky, the people left behind might throw some funeral games.

Running my hands over the smooth faces of Cape Cod gravestones, I am once again gazing at the inconceivable night sky, watching numberless water molecules rushing past me in a stream, staring out my window trying to count snowflakes.

I am small. I couldn't begin to remember them all, to know them all, and yet I yearn to. Each of theses stones marks the final page of a novel, a page with nothing but FINIS, centered and lonely. Only a good novel can make me enjoy the final page. With the best of them, especially with the best of them, that last page is bittersweet.

I want to meet every one of these dead fellow cast members of mine. I want to feel their grips and watch the lines around their eyes when they smile. How many died peacefully, happy with their end, always knowing that it would come at sea? Or maybe they were surprised that it hadn't, amused that those remaining behind would actually have a body to plant.

Spring sun and spring rain mixed us our weather while my wife and I spent those days wandering on the cape. I watched the tomb-sea, thinking about the coldness of that death, wanting to be given a number, wanting to know how many dead it held, how many continents held more.

Driving up the Massachusetts finger, we found a small but official-looking building set out near the dunes. Wind and rain pushed us toward it.

Inside, a smiling man pointed to a miniature theater.

"The movie's starting," he said. "It's about whaling."

Alone, we laughed in the uncomfortable seats. The screen found its life, and suddenly we were looking at the faces of the dead.

Brown, flickering, hand-cranked just faster than time's

normal speed, men move around on the deck of a whaler, the last North American whaler. Or so we are told.

Men missing legs and hands, men with salt-hardened faces that had begun dying the day they were born, scurry and clamber.

Longboats and harpoons—the time we are watching is as dead as the people. A great carcass is strapped along starboard, and a man climbs down onto its back. Sharks churn in the water while he, alone, severs the whale's head.

Brought on board somehow, the head is positioned with its cavity facing us, and a one-armed man ladles out the precious oil from the whale's skull. Where is *his* blank grave? He smiles at the camera, at the new and strange thing, a memorial that will remember him longer than stone, longer than any of his flesh and blood, a memorial that will flicker at strangers when they wander in from the dunes.

A narrator tells us that this ship and crew took only one more voyage. Caught by a storm, the ship, like thousands before it, was strewn across the bottom and broken over sandbars. All souls lost.

The old man with his ladle. The boy, eager and quick on the rigging, new to the sea. The shark-brave sailor.

I have a memorial to those men that hangs on my wall. I bought it just outside the theater. It is a map with lists and lists of the cape's known shipwrecks—"maritime disasters" according to its label.

The ships have names and dates. But for the men, there are only numbers. Souls counted. 125. 207. 34. No names and ages and short biographies. No mention of wives or mothers.

Now livelihoods are more easily made on the cape. Cranberries are farmed, and there are tourists to purchase pirate kitsch.

Strangely, the mortality rates haven't gone down. Everyone still dies. But now the novels have more (if less interesting) pages. It takes longer to reach FINIS.

I was young when my cousin was buried. She had taken some sort of shock to her brain during birth. She couldn't live without machines powered by dams that were holding back rivers. Or so the doctors said.

Her new cord, the cord powering the pump that was powering her lungs, was pulled from the wall. Her brain was dead, but her body, her soul, fought on.

For her the miracle of breathing was more obviously miraculous. Each one sounded like her last, each one of every day, all the way into her second year.

And then, late one night, my uncle got out of his bed on impulse and went and stood beside hers. Her body, tense and struggling since birth, relaxed. Her last breath came, and it was the only peaceful one that she had ever drawn.

Alexa was planted. Her spot has been marked. We will not forget her.

Not until we are forgotten.

◆

Denying God's power might quiet the nerves of some, but I truly cannot begin to understand why. When the roller coaster inverts me, twists me, and sends me into a tight spiral, I do not struggle philosophically or religiously with the idea of someone being in control or of engineers having been involved or of all of this being in some way intentional. As I quease and scream, do not stroke my cheek and try to reassure me by pointing to a panicking carnie as he wiggles powerless controls. Don't start holding my hand, telling me about the engineers' good intentions, but the impossibility of them actually knowing what the ride was going to do or where it would end when they'd created it.

In those stories, vomiting is my only option. And preferably on you.

Are we on a world kick-started by a god who doesn't know how to drive? Is this god embarrassed? Did he not know that snowflakes would come with avalanches as well as the quaint village scenes they ruin?

Of course He did. This God is big, bigger than the world. Faith is hard on the back of a motorcycle, it is hard when the Tilt-A-Whirl reverses its spin, when the bright lights blur into confusion against the night sky. But faith brings with it the only possibility of peace and joy in this world—the only possibility of laughter on this mad, mad ride.

Denying God's power is a theological attempt to reduce whatever sentence Man might choose to impose against Him, to cut down on Man's cosmic bitterness when the story goes dark. But if an all-powerful God is somehow made evil because He has given me pain, an impotent God is tainted in the same way.

If killing me makes an omnipotent God guilty of homicide, the best a partially potent God will get off with is negligent manslaughter.

What are our options? Who started this world? Are we talking about a God involved in creation in any way? Or are we simply talking about some macro-evolved being that we've somehow confused with management?

If God is the creator God, then He bears responsibility. If He is the cause, the Artist of all reality, then what is on His canvas points back to Him whether He put it there with the meticulousness of a Dutch Master or dumped cans of paint into a fan like some undergrad artist desperate for grant money. If there is guilt to be had (which is a rather large *if*), then both share in it. If you have some standard of evil bigger than God is, a courtroom big enough for Him to be tried in, and the authority to charge Him, then by all means do so. We can discuss His defense and jury selection later.

But if God is the creator God and He was somehow unaware of what He was starting, unaware that the Holocaust was going to happen, shocked when He first heard of Hitler's plans, and embarrassed that He couldn't stop him, then He still remains the first cause of all evil. He began a chain of events beyond His control.

"But it wasn't on purpose (wring hands here). How was He supposed to know how fast everything would go to hell? He expected people to act more like Strawberry Shortcake."

Don't think this would get Him an acquittal. He might not like the world-accident He began, but He should have known better. If anyone could be expected to know better, it's God. Had He been drinking? I'd go with an insanity plea.

God was the first to cry. Is this comforting? He's the first to get bad news. If only He were just a little quicker. Or maybe, "You know, He's really sorry. When He invented fire He didn't realize that it could burn skin. I hope you remember everything He's said about being forgiving. Apply it now."

Of course, the nonexistence of God is nothing more than a nonsense option. The categories of good and evil themselves require some sort of transcendent standard. What makes things good? What makes things evil? Atheists have, by and large, given up on the idea of an absolute standard of morality. After all, spiritual emptiness and the nonexistence of anything outside of the simple material universe is no way to come up with an ethical system. Morality is cultural preference (which cannot be said to be right or wrong) and fundamentally relative. It takes on (to be generous) the same authority as Wisconsin speed limits on a Nevada highway at night.

People are raped in this world, and rape is evil. Because evil exists, there must be no God. Because there is no God—no authoritative standard over creation—the badness of rape downgrades to a mere matter of societal taste. Ethnic cuisine, ethnic ethics. In God's absence rape is no longer fundamentally evil. In our country, you'll get confined to a cell (if caught and convicted), but that just means we enforce our taste, not that our taste has any real authority over anyone else. In other societies, girls have been passed around and traded like baseball cards. Is that right?

Is that wrong? Neither. You like exploitation; I like apple pie. The two discussions exist on the same plane. There's no such thing as moral and immoral. In this country, we eat gyros. In this one, we eat pizza. And we'll give you a ticket for jaywalking.

Stunning. Such wisdom is like a kiss on the lips.

To quote one contemporary prophet: "You and me, baby, ain't nothing but mammals, so let's do it like they do on the Discovery Channel."

I've watched the Discovery Channel. I've enjoyed the Discovery Channel. But in that world, if I want to reproduce with you (or tear you limb from limb), I just need to be bigger and stronger than you are. You look pretty small and a little sickly. Shall I feed you to my young? Why not? Cannibalism might not be condoned in your culture, but it has a long and storied tradition in mine. Are you saying your culture is superior, that it is somehow right while mine is wrong? You're being a racist, but luckily you're still small, and even racists taste good in casserole.

In some beehives, there is a point in the early phases of winter when the worker bees rebel. They begin laying eggs of their own, unfertilized eggs that will still hatch (oddly), but only into males. The queen is enraged and eats the eggs of her ladies in waiting as fast as they can lay them. They are desperate for their own young and lay as slyly as they can, but to no avail. The queen devours on.

Finally, despairing and frantic, the workers turn on the queen, stinging her to death. Winter falls on this civil war. Not one bee will survive until spring.

I could never believe in a God who would allow such darkness, who would allow bees to feel pain and frustration, who would allow Russian novels to play out in the insect world. Let alone in Russia.

Nietzsche was honest. He understood that it was not a matter of disproving God's existence, so much as disliking Him. Whether God existed or not, Nietzsche didn't care. From *The Anti-Christ*:

> The thing that sets us apart is not that we are unable to find God, either in history, or in nature, or behind nature—but that we regard what has been honored as God, not as 'divine,' but as pitiable, as absurd, as injurious; not as a mere error, but as a crime against life. . . . We deny that God is God. . . . If any one were to show us this Christian God, we'd still be less inclined to believe in him.

True atheism is nonsense. If there is such a thing as beautiful, such a thing as good, or even such a thing as bad, then there is a transcendent standard that determines which is which. An atheist can say that society prefers mothers to murderers, but he cannot say that this is as it *should* be. Tell us what *is*, by all means. But without God, you cannot tell us what *ought* to be.

An atheist can tell us that he is a good person, that he has never stolen a lawn mower or murdered his wife. I believe him. What he cannot tell me is what is fundamentally wrong about lawn mower theft and wife killing. He will try, but he can't change the fact that in his world there is no such thing as fundamental wrongness.

Let the man with the biggest armies and the booming voice make the rules. Jews and gypsies and homosexuals be damned.

I don't like that picture. I look at the world and I see beauty. I see love and loss, birth and death, joy and sorrow. I see a world where color exists, and in enormous generosity we were given eyes to see it. This is a world where bread makes a smell as it's baked, and we just happen to have noses to smell it. Color, smell, sound, taste—these are things that could have gone unnoticed; we could have been senseless in this reality, careening around like so many spattering particles. Were our noses invented first, or the smells? Our eyes, or the sights? Breasts, or desire?

We have been created as recipients. I look at the stars, at the grass, at my fat-faced children, at my fingernails, and I am oppressed by gratitude.

I have been given a belly so that I might hunger. I have been given hunger so that I might be fed.

I look in the atheist's mirror. I look at his faith in the non-existence of meaning. I look at his preaching and painting. I see nothing but a shit-storm.

Why would I walk through that door? Why would I live in your novel?

◆

William of Occam thought he'd derived a helpful principle from the universe. It has been called his razor.

All else being equal, the simplest answer is the truest.

But why should simplicity be king? Where do you see simplicity in this world? Do we need to return to probabilities and likelihoods? Do you need me to convince you that you can't possibly be here?

In Virginia, there lived a man named Roy Sullivan. He was struck by lightning seven times. I'm told the rough odds of this happening are out of 1.6×10 to the 25th (sixteen septillion). Which is like one man winning a state lotto four times, though the luck is of a different stripe. Find me the simplest explanation.

Did Roy believe in God? Did he like Him?

In 1983, at the age of 71, he killed himself. The lightning had nothing to do with it. Rumor was (according to Reuters) that he'd been jilted in love.

◆

Three postcards await our perusal, yea, three visions of a world.

One: I see a theme park where there are lots of rides, but there is nobody who can control them and nobody who knows how the rides end. Grief counseling, however, is included in the price of admission.

Two: I see an accident. An explosion of some kind inhabited by happenstantial life forms. A milk spill gone bacterial, only with more flame. It has no meaning or purpose or master. It simply is.

Three: I see a stage, a world where every scene is crafted. Where men act out their lives within a tapestry, where meaning and beauty exist, where right and wrong are more than imagined constructs. There is evil. There is darkness. There is the Winter of tragedy, every life ending, churned back in the soil. But the tragedy leads to Spring. The story does not end in frozen death. The fields are sown in grief. The harvest will be reaped in joy. I see a Master's painting. I listen to a Master's prose. When darkness falls on me, when I stand on my corner of the stage and hear my cue, when I know my final scene has come and I must exit, I will go into the ground like corn, waiting for the Son.

I see my world.

In *The Silver Chair*, the Marsh-wiggle Puddleglum is all wisdom in rebutting the witch as she denies the existence of the world in which he believes. But as children's fiction isn't quite academically respectable, I'll pretend that I learned this from Blaise Pascal.

What if I am wrong? What if Option One is as true as true gets and God is helpless at the controls of the world He built? Well, then I will be guilty of overestimating God. To put it even more strongly: I idolized Him. Oh, well.

As for Option Two: If the world really is accidental and devoid of meaning, and you and I have no more value in the cosmos than your average bread mold, and Beauty and Goodness are artificial constructs imagined within an explosion, constructs that are controlled by chemical reactions within the accident and have no necessary correspondence to reality, then my made-up children's world licks your real world silly. Depart from me. Go drown in your seething accident. Puddleglum and I are staying here.

Does David Hume deserve a straight answer on the problem of evil? He offered us meaninglessness, and in exchange, we gave him a tomb in Edinburgh. He has a statue as well. It is appropriately tarnished and quite official. He sits, swathed in a toga, revealing a soft chest and propping a tablet on his knee. He is dead, and his statue is easy to ignore, but his complaints live on. They lived before he did, and they live now. As long as there have been Christians, this argument—evil as evidence of an absent or nonexistent God—has been hollering at them from the middle of the field, swaggering like Goliath. But is it a Goliath? It looks angry enough, threatening enough, but it seems smaller, more like a five-foot-nothing Nietzsche than a Philistine giant.

What does he weigh? A buck ten? Have we tried hitting him with a rock?

How could an all-good, all-powerful God allow evil in the world? Or, from a slightly different angle: how could an all-good, all-powerful God allow David Hume in the world?

I hate to do it, but to answer the question, we need to know what evil is. And we need to know what standard exists that distinguishes it from good.

Is it that hard to define? Isn't this just another place where philosophers put on their tight pants and do slow important jigs? Well, yes, actually, it is. But we can do it faster and hope to be less silly. Or maybe embracing the silliness is a better route.

St. Augustine proposed that evil was an absence of good,

what he called a privation. Evil did not exist as a thing but was used as an adjective to describe those actions that lacked positive virtue. This way, as evil did not have independent being in the world, God was not tainted by it.

Farther east and less Christian, you'll find theories of good and evil that should remind you of Star Wars. Good and evil are impersonal forces, holding each other in balance. Pursue the balance. A surplus of goodness might necessitate a tsunami. In many systems evil is equated with disorder or chaos. Good is that which is ordered and regular. In these, creation is often a matter of carving, shaping, or otherwise taming primal chaos. That underlying madness is always trying to break free, giving us "evil."

In the *Euthyphro* (one of Plato's little skits), the question is pushed from a different direction. Do the gods love that which is good because it is good, or is it good because they love it? Which came first, the ethical chicken or the ethical egg?

But Hume is specifically criticizing the Christian vision of the world, the idea of a creating God giving us this reality— shadows and all. On the Christian canvas, in the Christian story, what is evil?

Sidenote: Ultimately, this is an exploration of a position held in faith. Hume's criticism is that the tenets of Christianity are not internally consistent with themselves. Faith is inevitable and good, but faith in contradictions is useless.

Because God is good, because He is infinite, because He is perfect, because He is ultimate and no standard exists above

Him, evil is that which displeases Him. Evil is not something that exists like a goop creeping through the seams of reality. It is not a Force that can make you wear a black cape, a helmet, and give you asthma. Evil is an adjective. It is an adjective used to describe those actions of man (and their effects) that are contrary to the nature of God. To answer Plato's question with the inevitable paradox that such chicken/egg queries demand (especially when dealing with the infinite): God has always been. God has always been good. Therefore goodness has always been. He is the living standard of goodness, and so things are good when they are like Him. And He loves them because they are good—which was inevitable given that they mirror His nature.

Is that clear? Maybe I should have just gone with, "Both."

Since (in the Christian system) God is the standard of good and evil, the question can be reframed. How can an all-good, all-powerful God allow things in His creation that displease Him? And we can throw Leibniz in here for extra spice.

Given God's perfection, is this really the best of all possible worlds? Does the best of all possible worlds include people like David Hume?

In the Christian world there are a few favorite answers to these questions. Some thinkers give Leibniz a yellow ribbon for having been on the right track, but he is retooled. This is not the best of all possible worlds, but it is the best of all possible ways to the best of all possible worlds—namely, Heaven.

Connected to this answer is the response to the business of evil. Evil exists in the world because God created man as a free agent. With freedom (obviously) came the ability to do both right and wrong, to please and displease God.

But what a price. Why is human freedom so important that billions of lives had to be sacrificed on its altar? Because a Heaven populated by free souls is a better world than a Heaven populated by puppets. And because God is perfect, He had to build Himself the best of all possible worlds.

Or so the answers go.

But freedom, much as I am grateful for it, is not a good in and of itself. It depends on what is done with it. A free do-gooder is obviously better than a puppet do-gooder. But a puppet do-gooder seems far superior to a free serial rapist. A race of well-behaved puppets (from my humble critical standpoint) is something that I would prefer over a race of free Scythians pursuing their natural appetites among the women of the nearest village.

As Scythians have existed in this world, both literally and figuratively, I assume that they serve a better purpose than a mere monument to the side effects of human freedom.

What is the best of all possible feelings? What is the best of all possible things? The best of all possible creatures?

Clearly, the best of all possible feelings is the one that comes when the agony of too much time in the car with an overextended bladder has finally been alleviated. Such sweet relief remains unparalleled.

The best of all possible things is obviously a toothpick. Or a solar system. Are solar systems things? Do they qualify? What are we talking about?

The platypus is quite clearly the best currently living creature, but it is not the best of all *possible* creatures. In addition to its mammalian, egg-laying, duck-billed, web-footed, amphibious life, it also could have had bat wings, sonar, and the ability to fire explosions out of its rear like a bombardier beetle. To speak frankly, I feel that a creative opportunity was missed.

The best of all possible . . . what? Worlds isn't enough. What kind of worlds are possible? What are we comparing it to? To what end? Which is better, a hammer or a thermos? A knife or a peanut?

I don't know; what's the goal? What is the world for? If we knew that, then we might get somewhere.

If the goal for this world was to give us easy skiing into immortality, then I'm afraid the user evaluations will be scathing. If the world was meant to be a pleasure palace, where no sensations ever quite reached the point of being painful, then this is a flop. I stubbed my toe on Saturday. On Monday a large man with neck acne elbowed me in the forehead. My skull remains sensitive, but that doesn't hurt nearly as much as knowing that he ruined my best of all possible days. I was on a good run. However, the blow was sturdy, punishing, and yet did no permanent damage (not that I would notice). In addition, it was perfectly centered on my head, rose up in pure symmetry as the swelling grew, and there was even a little bloody pucker where the skin had broken directly in the middle of the lump.

It was quite potentially the best of all possible nonfatal but disturbing elbows to the head of an author who should be writing a book but is playing basketball instead. I congratulate it.

What is the world? What is it for?

It is art. It is the best of all possible art, a finite picture of the infinite. Assess it like prose, like poetry, like architecture, sculpture, painting, dance, delta blues, opera, tragedy, comedy, romance, epic. Assess it like you would a Fabergé egg, like a gunfight, like a musical, like a snowflake, like a death, a birth, a triumph, a love story, a tornado, a smile, a heartbreak, a sweater, a hunger pain, a desire, a fulfillment, a desert, a dessert, an ocean, a leap, a quest, a fall, a climb, a tree, a waterfall, a song, a race, a frog, a play, a song, a marriage, a consummation, a thirst quenched.

Assess it like that. And when you're done, find an ant and have him assess the cathedrals of Europe.

This painting is by an infinite Artist. It is a reflection of Himself (could there be a better subject?), worked out in colors, lives, and constellations, in a universe that to us seems endless but is to Him a mere frame, a small space, a confining challenge for His artistry.

The temporal narrative of reality is every Art—invented and collected and woven into one cosmic, finite portrait of the infinite. Bring in the bricks and let them criticize the city.

We would work with less wood, they say. And we're not sure if concrete and steel really connect enough with the motif of civilizations as organisms.

Bring in the grasses and hear how they could improve upon the world.

The trees are pompous, and prairies are underrepresented. We'd like to see the oceans reduced. Or perhaps a floating prairie could be arranged. We'll submit designs. And whoever approved the cattle concept should be fired.

Where would you improve it? Flying cars? Fewer elbows to the head? Rebirth as a British royal? A shift in what most beautiful women want in a man? Time travel?

Good ideas. Definitely. Pass them along.

Perhaps you feel a more serious burden. Looking out of your eyes, the world could easily be improved. Fewer people could die. Death could be banished. Hunger slaked. Thirst quenched.

Evil, that which displeases God, should be gone.

So it should. But how? When? What is it that you are assessing? Would *Pride and Prejudice* be improved by throwing away every page prior to the resolution, by erasing every character flaw, every misunderstanding and dispute?

Ansel Adams once took a photograph he titled "Jeffrey Pine, Sentinel Dome." It is beautiful. He stood where he did, he saw what he saw, and he was able to catch it, fitting it into a small frame with only two dimensions and nothing but blends of black and white. The sky is there, the rock, the Jeffrey Pine.

The tree grows on the left, but it is gnarled, bending even now, spreading across the picture in its struggle against the wind. Its muscled branches are frozen in their strain, unquivering; its roots claw into stone, matching granite strength. There is a mountain watching from a distance, wondering who will win. The tree has fought for this life, fought in this permanent unretreating retreat.

The wind will win in the end, but this uncomplaining tree is noble. I see no bitterness, no resentment. We may forget, but this tree knows that the world is spinning, and it has hung on to the globe through decades. I see pride in those roots, gratitude where the light sits.

Could we improve this picture? How can we make it not better but *best*? Remove the tension and the contrast. Remove the black. All of it. Remove the struggle and the inevitable end.

Leave the white. Only white. And now it is perfect. Perfectly blank.

If we live in art, struggling in the boundary between the shadow and the light, unable to see the whole, how can we begin to judge? How can we presume to talk about a better painting, a better novel, when we see only a single line, a single page, and it brings us grief?

Any single needle can complain. There is death in those branches. Surely I could be full and green, surely I need not be in the wind, connected to the struggle? There is a shadow sprawling across me. I am cold. Can we bring in more light? The contrast could be softer.

And so we all speak. Each of us wanting our own position a little more comfortable. Each of us wanting to see a little more happiness, a little less contrast, wanting to skip the struggle, throw away the novel and save only the final page, the FINIS. A world of tombstones would have no wars, no hardships, and no complaints. So would a world without births or loves or creeping, crawling, walking, or growing things. A better artist would have made this world more like the moon, only without the black space behind it, without the contrast of edges. A sprawling, near-infinite moon. Erase the craters.

The painting is blank. The art is numb. Perhaps it is the best of all possible numbness.

St. Paul made his point: Cannot the porcelain maker choose roles for his art? Can the toilet complain because the vase holds flowers and its breath is sweeter?

Imagine a speck of dirt denying the existence of God because it has been called to clog your pore. Imagine you denying the existence of God because you have pores that can be clogged.

After the fourth time Roy Sullivan was struck by lightning, he allegedly told a reporter that a higher power was trying to kill him.

That's ridiculous. A higher power was not trying to kill him. That would have been easy. Every last one of us is bagged in the end. The more impressive trick is striking someone with lightning seven times and keeping them alive.

Have you ever had something so annoying happen, something so impossibly coincidental, that you know there must be a God, and that He must be laughing? Do you want to be the character

in the movie who can't take a joke, who can't laugh at the awk-
ward, at the uncomfortable? Worse, the character who can't
laugh at himself?

If you discover one morning (with moist toes) that the toilet
bowl has been covered with plastic wrap, do you deny the existence of your roommate?

Ask yourself this question: who invented your roommate,
and decided to give him a role (along with certain impulses and
sensibilities) in your life? Complain. Whine. Be a fusser. The
story needs those as well, because every butt needs a joke, and
the audience must laugh. Whether they (and God) laugh *at* or
with is up to you.

There is a church in Oxford that has been standing for lifetimes.
There are many such. But it was to this church that my wife and
I walked, crowded under the same umbrella, in a caravan of
cousins and family. Spring was far away while we wound through
the small streets, picking a course through the cold air, guided to
a cold stone sanctuary.

Living people worship here now, but they are far outnum-
bered by the congregation of the dead, outsung by the voices of
eight centuries.

We add our echoes to the place, a place worn smooth with
worship. The rain has stopped and we release our children into
the garden, a lumpy place, mottled with struggling grass in
hibernation.

Laughter and church clothes and muddy ground. Tea cakes
and coffee. I eat and talk and watch, but something seems strange.

There is a stone in the garden, near the edge, and another in a corner.

My sister stands beside me. This is her church. I look at her quickly, but she doesn't need to hear my question.

She nods. "They took out all the gravestones. It's hard to find room for a lawn in Oxford."

I have nothing to say. Not at first. Below the ground are the seeds, older than my country. Above them, my children play tag. It is not a crop they can harm, and we'll be gone, hiding in our own rows, before the Spring comes.

The world is no photograph. Evil is not a fixed shadow hiding a branch, it is not the wind pulling forever at life.

In this story, the sun moves. In this story, every night meets a dawn and burns away in the bright joy of morning.

In this story, Winter can never hold back the Spring.

Every soul waits in the wings. Every life taken in age, tired and ready, taken in youth, in shock and sorrow, taken in pain or taken in peace, every needle now hidden in shadow waits in eager silence. I see my cousin. My nephew. Many faces, forgotten by those who followed behind, known always by the Author who needs no stone reminders. He is the best of all possible audiences, the only Audience to see every scene, the Author who became a Character and heaped every shadow on Himself.

The Greeks were right. Live in fear of a grinding end and a dank hereafter.

Unless you know a bigger God, or better yet, are related to Him by blood.

The last page approaches, reached only through trials and triumphs, tears and laughter. The ending comes. But God is too big for endings, too big to work with a single narrative arc. This will be the end of Death, the end of a story that began in a garden and has played out in gardens ever since.

Let us bury Death in a garden, and seal the hole with a cross. For him there will be no Spring.

There is a rustling of impatience. Anticipation. Creation creaks and groans, tired of shadow, tired of Winter.

The sun comes.

The corn will see the morning.

Through the long cold, I wait for the Spring. I watch for it, but I never see the moment of its arrival.

The sun warms me, reminds me.

Be grateful, it says. I have broken the Winter.

On the south side of my house, the crocuses are up in bunches. They are the most greedy for spring, the first to notice and explode.

Daffodils will follow soon.

After them will come the sailors.

THE PROBLEM OF EVIL
AND THE NONEXISTENCE
OF SHAKESPEARE:
A PAPER BY HAMLET, PRINCE OF DENMARK

The spring is young and already people are coming out of hibernation, wandering the sidewalks with bare arms, exposing the remaining stores of winter fat to the sun's light. Some are too eager, shivering in shorts, blotched and mottled when they walk in the shade, pinking in the sun.

I sit in my car, two back in a growing line, waiting on a light.

I yawn. Cobwebs cling to my mind. The occasional cloud dims the day, and diesel from the truck in front of me keeps my window up.

Work waits for me at home.

There are times when it is easy to go numb, when it is easy to forget that you sit in a box of metal, dug from the earth and alloyed, shaped by the men and robots of Detroit. I don't care that I sit three feet above the ground in a machine with the soul and strength of (muffled) explosions. Horses are for recreation; my harnesses are hitched to pounding bursts of fire, and they pull me (gently, please) without complaint, while I collect invisible waves from the air with a magic metal wand and turn them into orchestras, pop stars, and indignant voices complaining about the war. It is easy to forget that the trees are busily carving up the air with sunlight and factory-producing the new year's leaves more efficiently than Germans.

Yawn. Again.

It is easy to be numb to the world's marvels when you've missed lunch and the light is still red.

Faith quavers under such trials. Who cares for the cosmos? Who has time or energy to ponder the tides or the multitude of narratives in the world? My blood sugar is low. My stomach is empty.

My kingdom for some peanut butter.

God is less than inclined to provide signs and wonders on demand.

I sit behind the wheel and ponder the loaves and fishes. Looking at the borrowed book on the passenger seat, I pray, but apparently not in faith.

This book, this useless book, it exists only by the power of Your word. Tweak the art. You know it could be ham if You wanted it to. It could be an unending slice of honey-cured. You have only to speak and it will be. Wouldn't the world be a better place if there was just a little less hunger?

Forget your stomach, He says. Open your eyes.

There is a college girl on a BMX bike, and she's trying to cross the street. She's wearing a sorority hoodie and baggy sweats, but they can't hide the fact that she's a little bit . . . pleasant. And she's having trouble with the bike.

I watch, because it's more interesting than watching my red light. As traffic passes, she strains at the pedals, but they won't budge.

She's embarrassed, aware that she's in public, glancing at cars, nervously laughing. Riding off on some guy's bike had seemed like a hot idea, flirty even.

Cross traffic is slowing. Our light is about to change, and she hasn't even gotten off the corner. The cars in front of me are relaxing on their brakes, easing forward. The light turns, and we move in earnest.

So does the girl. Suddenly her bike gear catches, and she shoots out in front of us. Our brakes lock and tires whine as she wobbles into the intersection, her eyes wide, panic hanging out her open mouth. She can't stop. She can't turn around. She pedals hard.

I see it before it happens. She is only thinking of the traffic, not of where her ride will end. We're all stopped, all of us watching, all the drivers and passengers on the cross street watching too. She could slow down and coast to the corner. Instead, pumping hard, she reaches the opposite sidewalk.

There's no room to stop. Four feet of walkway before she reaches the white, painted brick wall of an office building.

She turns, achieves separation from the bike, and thumps into the wall.

Her sweatpants fall first, down around her knees, exposing large pink skivs and a fake orange thigh-tan.

She crumbles to the sidewalk, tangled in bicycle and cotton-poly blend. One middle-aged male pedestrian walks toward her, biting back a smile.

I sigh, newly spiritual, grateful for the edification, appreciating one girl's sacrifice.

Traffic moves on. Freshened. Joyful.

She's standing up now, red and laughing. I don't even need to feel guilty.

Bruises heal, but stories are forever.

◆

We are not done with evil. We have not finished pestering the philosophers. There is more to be explored within the Christian story.

If evil is that which displeases God, then it is not possible for Him to be evil. He is the standard, the ruler, the inch, the ethical metric system (assuming, of course, that the metric system isn't evil).

This is wordplay, but it isn't *just* wordplay. If there is an infinite creator God who spoke the universe into existence *from nothing*, then what standard of goodness and evil could possibly exist outside of Him? What could He be compared to? What scale exists outside His own creation, what entity to surpass Him?

An infinite God is I AM, and all else must be measured in terms of His nature, His loves, and His loathings.

But within a Triune Godhead, there is room for comparison. "If you have seen Me, you have seen the Father." And God can be compared to creation—to this place with crashing bicyclists and laughing motorists. It is, after all, His art, the stylized narrative revelation of an infinite personality. Every thread in history plays a role in His divine portrait.

Aeschylus should have known he'd have an interesting final scene. He was, after all, the founding father of Greek tragedy. Before Emo, before the existentialists, there was Aeschylus, preaching. He didn't fuss about meaninglessness, because he wasn't a white, middle-class kid with a comfortable life, no butt, and tight pants. He wasn't French, awash in despair after the horrors of World War II. He was just a Greek who saw the world as a meat grinder. He knew there were gods, and he knew that if you achieved greatness, they would notice you and cut your ass down. He was most likely the author of *Prometheus Bound*, a heartwarming tale about Prometheus, the titan who got himself chained to a rock and had an eagle eat out his liver every single day (don't worry, it always grew back in between). Disney might use the concept in their next princess movie.

Aeschylus, like all those ancient, occasionally stoic, and always doomed Greeks, built his stories around a hero's tragic flaw—that weakness that got them dead in dramatic fashion. He knew that every man had those flaws, those character cracks, and in great men, the gods would go at them with a hammer and maul.

Aeschylus and Roy Sullivan, international lightning-strike champ, would have gotten along.

Aeschylus had his own tragic flaw. He was too obsessed with tragedy, too quick to see darkness (though it's hard to blame him with the gods he had). Maybe if he'd laughed more, if he had watched more sunrises and skipped more sunsets . . .

One day, Aeschylus was walking, no doubt lost in his thoughts. Perhaps he was mentally outlining a story about a beautiful shepherdess who foolishly (though accurately) believed herself to be more lovely than several goddesses, got raped by Zeus for her trouble, and then was fed to a flock of starlings by Zeus's jealous wife.

Regardless of what was on his mind at the time, an eagle spotted Aeschylus's bald head, picked up a tortoise, and flew to a great height. The tortoise was released, and plummeted, confused—a shelled, reptilian agent of death.

One step to the left, one step to the right and things would have been different. A broken clavicle? A lost ear? Who knows how many more tragedies would have seen the stage if Aeschylus's own story hadn't found dark comedy.

Shell met skull, and Aeschylus, father of the unhappy drama face, founder of the eternally-eaten-liver genre, died of having a turtle dropped on his head.

Historians are silent when it comes to the turtle. Did it survive? Where did it go? Was it ostracized, unable to stay in Greece after offing a favorite native son?

We know what a killjoy is, but what should we call something that kills the tragic?

There is only One who knows what happened to the turtle that killed tragedy. Only One knows where it hatched and what sent it out into the open to keep a date with an eagle. Only One knows where its grandchildren are sheltering tonight and whether they are cheerful. Only One knows how each will find its own final scene.

Question: Would you rather die instantly, with a turtle beside you, leaving behind an amusing story to make chuckling audiences throughout millennia feel just a little bit guilty for their laughter, or be chained to a rock and have your miraculously replicating liver eternally breakfasted upon? Eagles are involved in both stories, but who was kinder to their character?

Hamlet was no atheist. God was very real for him, as was his own guilt. He did, however, come to the conclusion that the play in which he lived couldn't possibly be designed by an author, or in any way be intentional. His reasoning went something like this: If there is an author, then he must either be poor and lack control of his art, or he must be evil and malicious. How could a good and competent author ever allow such hardship in my life?

He has a point. Ophelia dies (to mention only one casualty). Why? She was an innocent, a bystander. What greater good did that death serve? Either the author disliked it and was unable to stop it, or he liked it and is a foul brute indeed.

The most satisfactory answer is clearly that there was no author.

If in David Hume's world David Hume had a soul, then it would be chuffing right now.

I, says the ghost of David Hume, certainly have more worth and value than Ophelia, and yet I am dead. She is nothing but words on a page.

The point is not to say that Ophelia is somehow as real as we are, or that every fictional character exists in some other dimension. The point is simply that the problem of evil leaves logic at home and goes out alone without a chaperone. The existence of evil in Hamlet in no way implies that Shakespeare lacked control of his art, or that he was evil. The implication that Shakespeare didn't exist is even more outlandish.

No doubt he wept for Ophelia, and his tears were not false.

David Hume, have patience. You're closer to getting a straight answer.

I see craft in the world. I cannot watch dust swirl on the sidewalk without seeing God drag His finger, or listen to spring rain running in the streets without hearing Him roll his Rs. For those who believe in an *ex nihilo* creation, the world is inevitably art, and it is inevitably art from top to bottom, in every time and in every place. The world cannot exist apart from the voice of God. It is the voicings of God.

And so the question shifts. The implications of creation

combined with the continued existence of reality necessitate ultimate craft, an omnipotent storytelling God.

But can this God, the God who made moths to worm my apples and birds to eat the worms; the God who allowed His characters to displease Him, to grieve Him; the God who allowed death and decay to enter stage left, who allows shadows in His paintings and damning flaws in His characters—can that God be good, let alone perfect?

Watch the news and wonder. Hear of tornadoes and eight-limbed babies, holocausts and harvesting accidents. Get lost in the starkest shadows in the photograph. How many souls were swallowed by the sea today? When will the next tsunami make war on Asia?

How can this Artist be good? Does He not know that we feel pain? That children hunger and die? That we devour each other and the world whenever we can? His hands must be tainted even touching this canvas. His tongue must be stained, rolling out these words.

Or there is no He.

And so Hamlet reasons, Hamlet with his deep grief and deep pain.

When I was sixteen I sat in a baseball dugout wearing a bright all-star uniform but watching others play. Another player sat beside me, the two of us alone with sunflower seeds and conversation through a string of games.

Frustration was real. Both of us wanted to play, but the

coach had reasons for our exclusion—profound reasons (according to rumor) that were based on old friendships and checks written toward uniforms. We were unwilling to consider skill as a factor.

Ted felt no guilt in his anger. He was the better athlete, more starkly superior to the player on the field who had taken his position. He stewed while we talked, and I leaned against his steam—it helped me lean against my own.

Things could be worse. Look at the sun, the grass, the sky. Savor your sunflower seeds, imagine the story that brought them here to your tongue, a story that spans thousands of years. Perfect your in-mouth shelling and expectoration.

It was a hard lesson for two first-world kids—comic that it should be.

I fought to make him laugh, to show him how small this trial really was. Eventually, I won. Together we laughed, and the dugout became more pleasant than the field.

"You're alive," I told him. "Even if you aren't alive in center field. You could be drowning right now."

"I could be burning alive," he countered, and spat.

I laughed. "True. But drowning is worse."

He stared at me, his eyebrows up, his hat pushed back on his head. Then he snorted. "No way. Burning would be way worse."

Right or wrong, I made my case. In fire you would be far more likely to pass out before any extreme agony. In drowning, however, you would be fighting, panicking, with lungs screaming to be filled, and then screaming when they were.

He resisted briefly, but in the end he was convinced.

We emptied bags and scattered shells, talking about death and souls, watching painful games, losses we couldn't do anything about.

When the final game ended, his anger returned. I left the dugout to find my father.

As we walked to the car (I in my untarnished uniform), I looked across the park. There was Ted, holding his bat, an expensive bat, cocking it back and unleashing the swing he hadn't been able to use, collapsing aluminum against the thick trunk of a tree.

I yelled at him while he pounded. He looked up, and I cupped my hands, reminding him where else he could be, that lungs aren't always full of life.

He turned and walked away.

How long was it? Two weeks?

Laughing with sisters, a newspaper pulled my eyes to black words in bold.

A local athlete had died.

I know the feeling I had when I read the headline, when I saw the name. I know it perfectly. I know, because I have it now. The tight throat. The unsure stomach. Hot eyes and a soul ache.

Ted had drowned, swimming after a few friends in a reservoir. A small reservoir. Almost a pond. He'd been there, and then he hadn't.

Eventually, divers found his body.

Tragedy isn't an easy thing to kill. It takes more than a turtle. Tragedy must be destroyed by someone willing to be swallowed by it, willing to be broken, torn out of the flesh, but able to return to it. Someone must be able to shatter the tragic from within and exit into comedy, able to rip a hole so wide that a train of souls, a parade, could follow after, banging drums and throwing candy as they strolled into the sun.

When my grandfather listens to Debussy's *Clair de Lune*, his stomach struggles. Darkness fires through his veins on impulse, pumped by a body with a long memory. As a kid, I watched him listen to my sister practice the piece, and I marveled at his stillness, his peacefulness, his shut eyes. The notes meant something to him that they could never mean to me. I asked, and he told me. In the war, he quieted his nerves with that piece of piano-shaped moonlight before his bombing runs. Death, explosions, faces lost in fire—those things attached themselves to the more soothing sounds, and the soothing sounds were overwhelmed. The soothing sounds became those things.

He moved through flight school with many other faces. Of his classmate friends, he was the only one still living when the war died.

I am here. You are here. Many others are not.

When will we join them? Will you go first, or shall I?

I have a chart in front of me, with bars indicating the probability of death for members of different age groups. It starts low and then climbs. Ten-year-olds are doing well in this country. But later on things get rough. Your probability rises like the tide until it is no longer a probability. It is a certainty.

What is the mortality rate for soldiers? For firefighters? For stay-at-home mothers and dentists?

What is the mortality rate for humans?

One hundred percent of people die.

When I was young, there was an egg that hatched into a larva that turned into pupa soup that became a monarch butterfly.

The butterfly lived a good life, though it never reached Mexico, the ultimate goal for every milkweed-feasting, golden-winged, flying decoration.

Before its migration had really even started, the butterfly was struck down by the antenna of our family car. Well, it wasn't exactly struck down. The very top of the antenna picked it out of the air, lining up its vertical shaft perfectly with the delicate creature's body. The bright wings folded back and met on the other side—a butterfly flag.

We let the flag fly for a while, and not even at half-mast.

Was God tainted?

Anteaters can consume more than thirty thousand ants per day. Thirty thousand lives, hopes, dreams, and aspirations. The anteater is a long-nosed destroyer of civilizations, taking more lives in one summer than Cambyses the Persian took in a generation.

If I could write an ant-story and have it played out in a mound, if I could shape a narrative and watch it lived by those tiny, teeming thousands, would I include any darkness? Would I include difficulty, struggles, frustration, and even death?

As the Spring grows, so does my grass. As the grass grows, rocks somehow make their subtle way around my yard, rocks that will damage my whirring blades when the grass is tamed, when its desire for world conquest is thwarted.

I pick up those rocks, and I throw them in the bushes.

For some creatures, six-legged and loyal, those rocks are the size of islands. I bend, with my son watching, and I jerk and pull until Manhattan rises up in my hands.

I will move Manhattan into the lilacs. I will watch it bounce and roll on the soft, newborn lawn and thump against the fence.

My son is impressed. He understands the momentousness of these spring decisions.

He knows what I've done, and he points to the small ants swarming in panic around our shoes. The rock was set deep. I've exposed pale dark-dwellers; the nursery chambers have been severed and crushed by my pulling. Other chambers, crowded with the unborn and their keepers, bounced across the yard in the clods clinging to the hurled rock.

A bird sits in the ash tree, watching, waiting for us to leave him alone with the wreckage and the refugees.

What is the death toll today, on this fine spring morning? What is the total number of living material things on this planet that transitioned into lifelessness between the hours of 8:00 a.m. and 12:00 p.m., PST? What is the global anteater population, and how many lives did they account for? How many thousands of tons of krill did the whales and seals and fish knock back today, and why are they worth less to the environmentally conscious than the whales? Is size the same thing as value? How many insects were eaten, how many birds, how many fish? How many bacteria died in my body alone this morning? I hope the number was high. How many viruses came to their final scene, lay down dramatically in embattled sinus passages, and delivered monologues suitable to their conflicted villainy?

David Hume, are you there? Knock on wood twice if you're listening.

My son and I still watch the ants, and I am unrepentant. I would not torture things for no reason. I would not throw an ant Manhattan into the lilacs without cause. I needed to mow my lawn.

Do the ants name these disasters? Are anteaters their tornadoes? Am I a tropical storm or a hurricane? Did their weathermen predict me? Do they still have their jobs?

These ants are functioning with an older system. As we watch, soldiers are dragging struggling earwigs into the center of the mound, earwigs rounded up from who knows where. Like every human civilization in the midst of disaster, they need scapegoats.

"Who tore down the sky?" the mob yells. "Who opened our world onto outer space? Who punched this hole in the ozone and brought the sizzling heat to our young?"

I can't tell which ants are the priests. I don't think the tiniest of BBC cameras could show me that, but I still hunch and watch, searching minute insect faces for some glimmer of authority.

If I could speak antish, I know what I would be hearing.

Lots of screaming, yes. But there must also be some codgerly old tunnel-dweller with stiff joints rolling his eyes and rattling antennae, clicking mandibles.

The cry goes up quickly once the word has been given.

"It was the earwigs! Their perverse unantlike ways and vile butt-pinchers have brought this upon us. The gods demand a sacrifice!"

The first earwig is decapitated.

"What are they doing?" my son asks.

"They're killing earwigs," I answer.

"Why?"

Two more are dead with their backs arching, pinchers splayed wide and clawing at the sky, asking the world, asking God why.

"Because they think it's their fault."

For a moment, I'm tempted to bring the rock back. I want to hide this little incident back in the sun-warmed soil. But it dawns on me that the sacrifices might be for me. They might know the earwigs had nothing to do with the devastation of their city; they must know perfectly well that I was the one who did it.

They think I want blood.

Here, take the souls of the earwigs. Leave our young. Put back the sky. How many do you want? We'll keep killing until your wrath's appeased.

I can't put the rock back. I can't lie to them like that. I won't stoop to fill the role of Zeus or the Aztecs' Quetzalcoatl.

"Kill as many as you find," I say out loud. "No earwig is ever really innocent. There are more in the mulberry bush with fat juice-filled backsides. And when you're done, move your civilization. I'll give you until tomorrow afternoon, and then I'm mowing the lawn."

My son looks at me. "They don't know our language."

I stand up slowly and look around the overgrown yard. "No they don't. But they'll be gone by tomorrow."

Who sinned, this man or his parents, that he was born blind?

Who sinned, this earwig or his parents, that he would be decapitated by ants?

Who sinned, this little bit of black oil paint or its parent elements, that it would be used by Rembrandt to do the dark, scary bits beneath the windmill?

If you are a glop of blue paint, blessed to be sitting in the sky overlooking Van Gogh's sunflowers, are you there by any effort or righteousness of your own? Why are you not more grateful?

I have a point. Let it be belabored and relabored. Is the horse dead? Hand me a whip.

In a world with evil, God is either not all powerful or He is not all good. Are these the only options?

Or He is Shakespeare, Rembrandt, Botticelli, Dostoevsky, Van Gogh (with both ears), Michelangelo, Vivaldi, Robert Johnson, N. C. Wyeth, and Gary Larson rolled into one.

Our art is tiny in comparison to His. Our personalities are tiny in comparison to His. And yet He says that we are in His image. He is infinite (what can that really mean to our minds?)

and the narrative of this universe, the song of this universe, the epic of this universe, the still-frames of this universe on every level—from quarks to galaxies—reflect His self, His character, His loves, His hates, His mercies, His judgments, His kindnesses, and His wraths.

This universe is a portrait in motion, a *compressed* portrait in motion, a miniature, inevitably stylized, for it is trying to capture the Infinite. The galaxies are each one fraction of a syllable in a haiku of the Ultimate. On the human level, art is all recompression, attempts at taking a sunset from the small frame of the horizon and putting it on a postcard; taking a blues riff, the rhythmic vibration of strings, and capturing a sense of loss; marble, chiseled and shaped until it shows nobility; a cartoonist's frame, simple ink, grabbing at six-year-old boyness, grabbing at laughter.

What is the best of all possible things? That which is infinite, always present and undecaying. That which is both many and one. That which is pure, ultimate, and yet humble. That which is spirit and yet personal. That which is just and yet merciful. Yahweh, God. Father, Son, and Holy Ghost.

What is the best of all possible Art? That which reveals, captures, and communicates as many facets of that Being as is possible in a finite frame.

Do you dislike your role in the story, your place in the shadow? What complaints do we have that the hobbits could not have heaved at Tolkien? You have been born into a narrative, you have been given freedom. Act, and act well until you reach your final scene.

There was a time when men and women understood death more fully, when mortality was never ignored. Men and women executed their endings better then. Some even planned for it—letters from the grave, long-winded last words like characters from Dickens.

Those men, good and bad, heroes and villains, knew their final scenes would come, and they knew they would be *scenes*. They, like Solomon, knew that we are but vapor, that we are here for but a little while. We must exit the stage, down through traps, and let others traipse and sing, love and lose, fight and struggle above us.

The problem of evil is a genuine problem, an enemy with sharp pointy teeth. But it is not a logical problem. It is an emotional one, an argument from Hamlet's heartache and from ours. It appeals to our pride and our nerve endings. We do not want to hear an answer that puts us so low. But the answer is this: we are very small.

The apostle Paul: Who are you, O man?

Nothing in the existence of evil implies that God must not be in control. Nothing implies that He does not exist (exactly the opposite—without Him, the category *evil* does not exist; all is neutral flux and entropy). The struggle comes when we look at ourselves in the mirror, a carnival mirror, a mirror that stretches our worth into the skies. Given my immense personal value, how could a good God ever allow *me* to feel pain?

Our emotions balk at omni-benevolence.

I have killed good people. I have orphaned children and have given villains a period of strength, a time for them to wax fat before they are struck down.

I have done all this in novels for children. Am I a murderer? A predator?

Of course not. Am I a puppeteer? I hope not. I imitate the world as best I can. I want my characters free, but my art fails. I am not as big as God, and my characters are so much smaller than His, so much more artificial. His, well, His can really pop their knuckles, really fill their lungs with air, really look goodness in the eye and spit at it. But He wasn't content with only that. He exists on two planes. He sees the story as He tells it, while He weaves it, shapes it, and sings it. And He stepped inside it.

The shadows exist in the painting, the dark corners of grief and trial and wickedness all exist so that He might step inside them, so we could see how low He can stoop. In this story, the Author became flesh and wandered the stage with Hamlet, offering His own life. In this story, the Author heaped all that He loathed, all that displeased Him, all the wrongness of the world, onto Himself. Evil exists so that He might be demeaned and insulted, so that the depth of His love and sacrifice could be expressed as much as is possible in the small frame of history.

He stood before ants, listened to the bickering of the priests, and allowed Himself to be dragged to the center of the mound.

There is water in the world that once flew out of the mouths of guards and flecked the face of the Word Himself. There is iron that once tore at His back and iron that once coursed in His blood before it fell to the stones, left for the small animals to feed on in the night. Animals were born and spent a lifetime before being slaughtered, having their hides tanned and cut into strips, interwoven with stone and glass and lashing the skin off the One Poet's back, baring ribs full of calcium. There are proteins still, somewhere in this world, that were used in His beard before soldiers clutched, not knowing how close their fingers came to the Infinite, and tore hard.

But there is nothing now made from His flesh decomposed. That seed sprouted long ago, the firstborn, sprung from the womb of death on the first real day of Spring.

We could say He cares nothing for our pain. We could say He is not good. We could say we don't understand why the sky isn't all rainbows and why the common cold exists. But we would be fools. And somehow, He would still like us.

How much do I care for these ants? I think I care. I'll stop to watch their wars. I'll buy my children documentaries—insect tributes. I won't crush them when I can help it.

But, if given the chance, would I be willing to become one of them? Would I be willing for them to drag me to the place of execution, taunt me, mock me, ridicule the gift I offered, a gift entirely beyond their comprehension? Would I be willing for the earwig, executed beside me, to add his insults to those of the ants? Would I be willing to die?

Hell no. Never. I have more self-regard than God does. I have less love for the characters beneath me.

It is hard, being given head colds. It is hard, getting hungry three times a day. It is hard to be dependent on air and water. It is hard to only have two legs and not be able to fly. It is hard knowing that I will die. Knowing that I am not allowed to stay in high school forever.

Every last material creature on this globe will come to an end. If God has the authority to invent sperm, to invent eggs, to invent DNA; if He has the authority to choose me out of a near infinite number of possible human combinations and call me into existence out of nothing; if He has the authority to choose my parents, my race, my birthplace, my height, my intelligence, the size of my tonsils; if He has the authority to design my teeth from scratch, then He has the authority to choose my end.

God has the authority to shape a soul with His voice, bind it to matter, and send it into history. And He has the authority to sever my soul from my body and call it to another part of the stage. He has the authority to reuse the matter from my flesh in daffodils. I'm not worried. I'll get more.

There is no evil in His voice calling us to cross the Jordan, whether He calls us singly or in droves. There is no evil when He tells us to lay our first flesh down, no more than when He sends a caterpillar into its cocoon.

When one of my characters dies—no matter what other character pulls the trigger, no matter what guilt is incurred by others in the story—on the transcendent level, the level outside the cloth cover and dust jacket, I am the one who kills them.

Does the problem of evil leave a bruise, a tender spot, slow to heal? Put your finger on it. Push hard.

When we die, wherever or whenever that might be, there will be other characters in the story with us, evil characters, good characters, and confused ants. But God is also there, shaping the story, off the stage and on the stage, closing a chapter as a turtle bounces, smiling while it does.

To His eyes, you never leave the stage. You do not cease to exist. It is a chapter ending, an act, not the play itself. Look to Him. Walk toward Him. The cocoon is a death, but not a final death. The coffin can be a tragedy, but not for long.

There will be butterflies.

I will die, and when I do—whether it be in my bed as age creeps over me, or struck by lightning, a meteor, or a UPS truck—when my body and soul find their divorce, His hand will be the one that cuts the thread and shows me the path He blazed through tragedy. His finger will point to the parade.

◆

The sun is bright. Spring is as much about the death of death as it is about new life. The two are the same.

The wind is fresh from the upper sky and still carries a bite, a reminder of what it was, a threat of what it could be again.

I am home, with one flight of half-curled steps before my porch.

I am alive. I have legs. I will run with them.

Surrounded by spring, by maple trees wearing the new downy green of infant leaves, with a stone wall mortared by songs of full-bodied moss, I stretch my legs, skipping steps.

Near the top, I catch my toe. Is that what toes are for? My body travels forward without my legs. The earth does what it's told and sucks me down. Shin against cold concrete, hands against stone, I reach the ground.

I snort and blink slowly. For good measure, in a sign of submission, I let my cheek rest on the top stair. Grit sticks to my skin.

And then I roll over. Who was this for? Where's the audience? If I've peeled a slice of my shin, tell me I brightened someone's day. Some sad paper boy, a bored housewife, a student traveler who finds more beauty in the canned noise of an iPod than in the wild feral noise of a spring day.

No one. Just me. And any ants I may have killed. I look up at the blue sky. Someone is playing with clouds like fresh-blown bubbles.

Shins were invented with this special capacity for pain. Rubbing isn't helping. Laughing is.

"Right," I say. "I refuse to take responsibility for that one. The stair clearly moved. It's not the tripping I mind; it's the cheating."

Are you in shadow? Are you in pain? Next to you, is Hamlet a happy man? Has the rock been lifted, removing the sky, tearing your life in half?

Do not cry to me. I can only cry with you. I will not die for you. I am still too young in the meaning of love. Talk to the Fool, to the one who left a throne to enter an anthill. He will enter your shadow. It cannot taint Him. He has done it before. His holiness is not fragile. It burns like a father to the sun. Touch His skin, put your hand in His side. He has kept His scars when He did not have to. Give Him your pain and watch it overwhelmed, burned away by the joy He takes in loving. In stooping.

In the end, when your life is of a different sort, your first flesh will be dust, and of your grief, not one grain of ash will remain.

Are you sick? Are you drowning? Are you another confused earwig, dragged off your mulberry leaf by a posse of malicious ants? Do you reach your end?

Wait for us. We won't be far behind.

SPRING HIATUS: BUTTERFLY LIES

Reverse the world's laps. I have a memory:

My son has got his socks pulled up and his white tennis shoes on. The turf is rough for him and even worse on this slight slope. Every lump here is an obstacle. He's plenty fast on level ground, but this is a new difficulty. The wife and then-baby are following behind, cheering him on. I've given him control of the expedition, the whole park and no guidance. He may lead as he chooses. He leads down.

I know the look in his eyes. I know what it feels like. Dogs get it, too—dogs and boys. The fences are down, the doors are open, the leash is unclipped. Magellan probably had that look before the scurvy. I've assumed that we would stop, that there would be some distraction—grass that needed picking, a rock, a dandelion—but we plow on. A distraction does come, and it's past us almost before we notice. The blond head is twisting in the wrong direction. I help him.

"Over there, Rory." I crouch, turn him, and point. "There's the butterfly."

It's mostly black and almost the size of a monarch, but it doesn't move at all like one. This thing is fast. There's no flitting; it's sailing, paddling in time, keeping surprisingly level altitude, never opening its wings completely. There's red involved in there somewhere.

"I want to hold it," Rory says. This black-dusted flier is doing loops at the top of the hill thirty yards away. The whole park has disappeared for my son. The Jet Ski butterfly is the only thing of interest. Simple freedom has lost its attraction.

"Hold it," he reiterates. I look at his mom and smile.

"Baby," she says to him, "butterflies don't like to be held." He's not listening, so I bend my philosophies down beside him. I am his father. I will speak truth like an oracle. I will explain the world to him.

"Buddy," I say, for I am wise, "do you see how fast it is? It won't let you touch it. It will be scared of you and fly away so fast. When you grow up you'll be faster. We'll get you a net, and then you can try and catch it."

His eyes are following the butterfly. It leaves its hill and crosses the park, passing beside us before returning to its hilltop. My son is considering my words.

"I want to touch it," he says. I am not believed. He is a skeptic.

And then the butterfly comes. It comes fast—it has no other speed—passing right over our heads. But it hesitates. It has not landed since we first saw it.

It lands now. Not in front of us, so we can see it and accuse it of being a large and strange moth, but closer, on a two-year-old chest, just up by the left shoulder.

There it preens.

Rory freezes. He does not need me to explain the situation. He knows how these things are done. His chin drops and he stares at it. There are no flowers on his shirt, no bright colors, but he has been chosen while a father, a mother, and a baby sister all stand around and stare. The divine joke stays. The punch line rests awhile, and then it flies away.

Rory laughs but quickly grows serious. We, his parents, are both talking, offering our congratulations, informing him, as if he did not already know, that this has been a neat thing.

"Again," he says simply.

"Rory," my voice is rather cheerful, "I don't think the butterfly is going to come back. But it was right there on your shirt. Did you see it there?"

"Yes," he says. "Touch it again."

What else did I say? I don't remember. I laid out the laws of reality. Butterflies and lightning do not strike twice. And then God spoke.

"Do you see this man?" He said to my son. "He is your father. Do not believe a word he says."

The second time the butterfly landed on his arm.

How many lies have I told him? I and the world both. I have

repented now. I no longer tell him that he can't touch the moon from my shoulders. I tell him to stretch, and I offer to run and jump. There may be a dragon in the mulberries. I make sure to check. And I look for fish under the couch.

It hasn't happened again, at least not with butterflies. But tomorrow, when the scent of growing grass has been dew-pressed back to the earth and small lower-class butterflies are sunning themselves by the tire swing, then I will ask to hold one.

YOUR MOTHER WAS A LIZARD

Summer—sun-cure the world.

Spring is the only season that doesn't die. At least not where I'm standing, which (using a Toxics Release Inventory tracking tool provided by the EPA) happens to be at a latitude of exactly 46°43'49" and a longitude of -117°00'05" (in case you ever need to find it again). It's a street corner. By a coffee shop.

Here Spring just grows and greens and warms, spreading life, wrapping us in her arms, until suddenly we realize that she's not a girl anymore. She's a woman.

A woman named Summer.

The world is still greening when the students leave this town. They leave us alone to watch the feral aphids make the sidewalks sticky with the fruit of their feasting. They leave us to watch oceans of barley and wheat find a soft wind-rippled adulthood and a gold rattling harvest. The students leave the full joy of spring's summer transition to the locals.

It's quieter that way, and we can listen to the leaves grow and the wheat combing the wind's belly.

Spring is spiritual. Resurrection always is. Summer brings the fruit of that resurrection.

The afternoon is warm, and I am alone on the corner, watching the blues in the sky blend deeper as they bend to the horizon. Grain elevators tower a block away, cylinders to house the gold we grow.

"Hi." The voice is female. I turn and look into the face of a dark-skinned girl. College-age. Pretty. She smiles and pushes a wheelchair even beside me. The voice is in the wheelchair.

"Hi," she says again. This girl may be in her teens, she may be in her twenties or older. Normal aging doesn't apply. Her neck fights to hold her head to one side. Her arms are small, maybe usable, but she isn't doing much with them. Her legs are decorative, flightless wings. She looks me deep in the eyes, pouring hers into mine, giving all of herself, searching, seeing something she must like—humanity? Another being in existence?

I smile. "Hi."

Her smile is wider. "Will you be my friend?"

"Yes." I laugh. "Sure." As I say it, I suddenly feel guilty. Do I think she doesn't understand what friendship is, that I won't be called on to keep my bargain? It was witnessed. A third party stood right here and watched me agree. I'm ready. If she asks me to come to her birthday, I'll be there. I'll bring the cake.

"Do you like the sun?" I ask.

"Yes." She shifts hard in her seat, leaning forward. For a moment I think she'll fall. I glance at her attendant. She's still smiling, quietly, with her face tipped up toward the sunlight. The girl is strapped in.

She twists in her seat and throws her head back. "Will you be my friend?"

"Sure," I say again.

"I like friends. I have lots of friends."

"I'm sure you do." She must have with that smile and such a quick pitch.

Her face scrunches in curiosity. "What's your name?"

The wheelchair moves forward into the empty crosswalk. The girl's attendant gives me one last tight-lipped smile. I give her a nod.

"What's your name?" the girl yells, still twisting back. Her voice is growing frantic. It's hard to lose a friend.

"Nate," I yell to her, and she turns to face forward, satisfied.

"Will you be my friend?" Her voice echoes off the fire station, but I don't need to answer. Someone else is walking toward her.

Someone about to make a friend.

Unless ye be as little children.

That girl and I both bear the image of God. But neither of us bears it completely. There are ways in which she is a truer picture than I can be, ways in which she sees the world new and fresh and undistracted by the past and the future. I have no doubt that while she looked at me, she loved me. Were I a better image, I could return such a favor.

But now she knows nothing of me. Her affection has flamed

and is pointed at another, or perhaps sorrow is with her now, as deep and instant and complete as her joy.

My gift is only in remembering, a gift pale and hollow next to hers.

I pitied her. Perhaps she pitied me.

Nietzsche published *The Anti-Christ* in 1888. Along with many other things, he had this to say about pity: "Pity thwarts the whole law of evolution, which is the law of natural selection. It preserves whatever is ripe for destruction; it fights on the side of those disinherited and condemned by life; by maintaining life in so many of the botched of all kinds, it gives life itself a gloomy and dubious aspect."

One year later Nietzsche entered into madness. True or false, the story is that he was overcome by the sight of a horse being whipped. Unhinged by pity. He wouldn't die until 1900. For a decade he was kept alive and maintained through his insanity, strokes, and incapacitating illness. At the age of fifty-five, partially paralyzed, unable to speak or walk, he discovered what life waited for him beyond the grave.

Nietzsche lashed out at his Maker with his tongue, the only notable muscle he had—his greatest gift. The Lord gives and the Lord takes away; blessed be the name of the Lord.

There was little that Nietzsche loathed more than the heritage of his Lutheran father.

I have never been irritated by Nietzsche, never annoyed. At his most blasphemous, at his most riotously hateful and pompous, I have only ever been able to laugh. But even then, there is something bittersweet about the laughter. I know his story. I know how his bluff was called, how he was broken.

Again from *The Anti-Christ*: "The weak and the botched shall perish: first principle of *our* charity. And one should help them to it."

Spake the paralytic. The man fed with a spoon by those who loved him.

"What is more harmful than any vice—Practical sympathy for the botched and the weak—Christianity. . . ."

And yet, because I see the world through my eyes and not his, I have sympathy for Nietzsche himself. Bodies and minds are not all that can be botched in a man. Souls can be hollow, twisted, thrashing, more bitter than piss.

Not all strangers in wheelchairs want to be friends.

While in grad school I met a man, scrawny, with a patchy beard, prime to be philosophical.

He smirked at my Christianity and spouted lines from the angry German who died gibbering. We stood in a soulless academic hallway and looked at each other. I'm afraid I didn't listen carefully. I was watching him eat while he talked, munching fries. I could see a burger box still tucked into the bag.

"What is rightness?" I asked. I'd interrupted a train of thought. He chewed and raised his eyebrows.

"Whatever comes from strength. Evil comes from weakness."

"Give me the fries," I said quietly.

"What?"

I straightened up and stepped toward him. I had at least six inches on him, and more than fifty pounds. "Give me the damn fries. The burger too."

I was ready to hit him, to throw him against the wall. Panic bubbled in his eyes, but I couldn't follow through. Laughing, I stepped back. He stayed long enough to blaspheme, and then he moved down the hall. His fries went with him.

I wish all Nietzsche's disciples were as small.

The world is seen in many different ways, but those who see Chaos as their father are the most confusing to me. I stare into their eyes, like a girl in a wheelchair, and try to sense any real difference in what they're seeing.

Have you noticed the dragonflies?

They've noticed the dragonflies.

They can't really have noticed. Did they see the nymphs? Do they know how they swim?

They've seen the nymphs.

But they're like jet boats. They pressure-fire water out their anuses. That's their propulsion.

They know. I know they know. We see the same things, and somewhere behind our pupils, those things become completely different.

Once, I accidentally threw a hot tub lid open onto a frog. I didn't notice until I shut it again. My sisters and I went wide-eyed. The creature was perfectly flat, and a puddle of moisture surrounded him. He'd been squeezed like a sponge.

We went to gather uncles and family, to collect witnesses for a memorial. When we came back the puddle was alone. The frog, freshly three-dimensional, sat on the edge of the lid, staring at us. He didn't even seem irritated. Possibly concussed, but not irritated.

If I'd been Catholic, and if I'd known the patron saint of frogs (Assisi?), then I might have lit a candle. Instead, I offered up the greatest thanks I had. I laughed.

The incident did not lead me any closer to agnosticism, and I think I can say the same for the frog.

If the world is fundamentally an accident, if in the beginning, there was no eternal personality, no eternal living being, merely super-hot, hyper-dense I AM matter (with no space and no universe outside of itself), and if, wandering those hyper-dense, super tiny corridors of the Forever Matter, attending to its normal routine, there happened to be one little chemical that caught its toe and flopped into another very different chemical, and both of them said, "Oh, crap," in tiny voices and went deaf in the explosion, then when did the accident start making sense and why the hell do we have the Special Olympics?

Is it strange that an impersonal accident should start talking about itself, that shards of matter rocketing through space/time would start making burbling noises and pretend that they're communicating with other shards, and that their burbling truthfully explained the accident? Is it strange to you that an accident would invent baseball and walruses and Englishmen?

If a hypothetical neutral observer had watched the birth of

an ever-expanding universe from the womb of an accidental fireball, was he (or she or it) surprised when the explosion invented llamas?

You see, for me, llamas are entirely consistent with the personality of an easily amused God. A prank on the Andes and everyone who ever needed to use the long-necked, pack-sweaters. Surly, pompous, comically unaware of their own looks, spitters. Perfect. Tell me a story about the great god Boom. Tell me how he accidentally made llamas from hydrogen.

Can we all be frank here? I know I'm not much like Elijah the Tishbite. No kings are after my head. I've never been fed by ravens or raised the dead, and I don't expect to be caught up to Heaven on a whirlwind. But Elijah spoke his mind with eloquence on the subject of the god Baal. He wasn't above a little earthy trash-talking.

As for me, I'd like to tell you what I think of this god, Boom. Do you serve him? Is Boom the creator? Then your god wets himself. Or haven't you noticed? It's all he's ever done. He's doing it now. Though, since he doesn't actually have personal existence, the atheist creator god is actually more of a process—Wetting Himselfness. In the annals of Boom, in the story of evolution, you, I, and both our mothers, are nothing more than creepy-crawlies somehow spawned (by lightning strikes, you say?) in a warm spot on the bedsheet of reality.

Okay, I know I'm not being fair. There is no god. Chaos has no personality. I'll grant all that. But the wetting part is fair. We, from sperm whales to constellations, are part of an agent-less accident—wet pants without the five-year-old.

Can we still be friends?

But what is friendship in an accident? And what's that smell?

Serve Boom, and you and I can still get along, but the way we see things changes everything. I see intentionality in the world, and so I imitate that in my art (and in the art I respect). You see a world that is no more than a large explosion, and the art that imitates that is a form of suicide.

One of the most important aspects of art is the relationship between a piece, between a canvas or a page, and its creator. I try to love what I shape the way I see God love His art. I, a glop of paint, a character on a stage, an extra in a musical, watch the care and love, sympathy and empathy He puts into every stroke, word, and bit of choreography. What I put on a page imitates, however clumsily, what He puts on His. But how I put it there is simply more imitation.

When Jackson Pollock created, he was imitating. He wanted his canvases to look like the world, and the world he saw was an accident, an explosion. But the world he saw wasn't actually art. It had no artist, and so he worked very hard to kill himself in relationship to his canvas. But he failed. He always failed, because he *was*, and that gave his art an artist—his own existence was a refutation of all he tried to preach.

He could punch holes in the bottom of cans and swing them from ropes, but he was still the one buying rope, arranging the canvas on the floor, and swinging. His art was never as accidental as reality. It was fundamentally false (in his world), because it had a creator—an advantage the Grand Canyon, Victoria Falls, the white cliffs of Dover, and the planet Jupiter didn't have.

Wim Delvoye is a Belgian artist. Who knows what he sees in the world? Currently, his greatest achievement is called *Cloaca*. It is a poo machine—shiny and efficient. Food is dumped into the machine (gourmet meals from top chefs while on display in New York), and after traveling through various baths of carefully balanced enzyme and bacterial digestion, it is squeezed into a three-dimensional vulgarity on a small moving belt.

You can buy the stuff in a vacuum-sealed plastic container (in case there's ever a shortage) and put it on your mantel. It comes with the artist's signature.

His shtick is the uselessness of art. See, see, I'm selling you something you already make for yourselves and totally dislike. There is no differentiation between the beautiful and the ugly. There is only useless and useful. Those things that are useless (like Handel's *Messiah,* a poo machine, a bit of chewed string, the Sistine Chapel ceiling, and tooth plaque) we call art.

While I stare at Wim's work, should I be surprised that I see things differently? This isn't useless at all, this long rack of tubes and enzyme buckets, this machine that cost thousands both in design and construction. How hard was this to make? How long did it take to get right? All of this, this factory of digestion, I have wrapped up in adaptable coils behind my navel. I never knew just how impressive that was.

Where are the battery coils on this machine? I want energy extracted from this food. I want to see something do jumping jacks thanks to this digestion.

It could be done—with thousands more in grants and further engineering.

I got all mine by accident in an explosion, prefabbed and intact by the time I was forced out of my mother's belly. Why don't you try that? It could be cheaper.

A question from uncited others: Would you ever expect to find the complete works of Shakespeare printed, collated, and bound by an accidental explosion?

But this is exactly what we have. An explosion that not only gave us the complete works of Shakespeare, but a bunch of bipedal units to act things out, crowds to weep and moan, and an industry of Shakespearean criticism that spans centuries. But the explosion didn't stop there. It also gave us Kafka, Russian architecture, solar panels, Jeffersonian democracy, Christianity, and ivory poaching.

We are bits of the flying flotsam, spinning away from the eye of the Great Disaster. Anything we do is attributable to Chaos, for we are its children, carbon-based shrapnel with sensitive nerve endings, a problem with self-importance, and a taste for pizza.

I see your painting. It's by Pollock. But where is your story? What is the plot? Who are the characters? What are the rules?

In this story, the Darwinian device that moves action is called (hail, the conquering hero) natural selection. But it has no purpose, no goal at all. Survival is the result for some and death for others, but there is nothing in this story to show that one is actually to be preferred over the other. Survival as *good* is just one of the axioms that's been adopted by the faithful. The characters? What do you mean? There is only a strange impersonal trinity— Time, Chance, and Matter. Matter exists, and it is shaped by chemical reactions as Time and Chance act upon it. You have no soul. You are simply a combination of chemicals. What you call "death" is nothing more than a transition out of one combination and the beginning of another. Welcome to the leaf pile—you as mulch is no better or worse than you as man. When *you* begin and end is a pointless question.

The polar caps are melting. Who cares? Let the great scurrying finish-lineless race for survival continue.

Costa Rican salamanders are disappearing? So? Stand with Nietzsche, not Christianity and its care and pity. Let the weak be trimmed. Let them and all the other weaklings, from bacteria to babies, be recycled into the strong and the hungry.

From C. S. Lewis's "Evolutionary Hymn":
Lead us, Evolution, lead us
Up the future's endless stair;
Chop us, change us, prod us, weed us.
For stagnation is despair:
Groping, guessing, yet progressing,
Lead us nobody knows where.

The truth is that very few academic atheists will try to maintain that atheism is pleasant. It has been pitched as a hard truth, and those squinty-eyed atheists are the brave ones (the "brights," according to Richard Dawkins), the ones willing to peer into the burning bosom of reality, see absolutely nothing, and write best-selling books about their experiences (and to convince us of our own soullessness). They preach this hard, chemically fatalistic doctrine like a bunch of Victorian Calvinists unable to understand why the populace won't simply bow their heads and come along quietly.

Because it is nonsense. (And you can keep your tenure. I'd rather have a ping-pong table.)

The Boom picture is uglier than mere paint spatters and a wandering, pointless, cosmic, global, national, state, and personal history. What is good and what is bad? Isn't rape an evolutionary impulse? Isn't trading in every postmenopausal wife for a fresh bit of breeding flesh a sound evolutionary move?

In the halls of graduate school, wisdom came to me through the mouths of dead oracles.

Immanuel Kant (all rise) gave us something he thought could be used to derive goodness and morality without God (though he was no atheist). That which was evil was so because it was irrational.

Kant's categorical imperative: Act only according to maxims which you can desire to be universal.

Student One: That doesn't make sense. It's a cheapened golden rule. Without a creating God imposing it, it's entirely arbitrary. Logic can't give you goodness, just validity. And if it could, how would a "rational" law achieve any actual authority in an accidental world?

Student Two rebuts: Think about bicycle theft. What if everyone stole bicycles?

Student One: We'd all have someone else's bicycle.

Is there something wrong with having someone else's bicycle? I do want to know.

Um, yeah. It's someone else's.

But what if I don't care? What if I want everyone to deny personal property rights? Does that make my theft okay? What if I want marriage done away with and sexual taboos tossed, and so I work hard to fit adultery and rape into my busy days? What if I want anarchy? Should I start shooting?

Of course not, you should pursue the greatest good for the greatest number.

Introducing . . . the ethics of gang rape and racial oppression. Goodness by majority rule has always gone well in the past. Just make sure there are more people enjoying the show than there are actually being fed to the lions.

Futility. Kant, well-intentioned egghead, gave us a logician's Golden Rule, and it lacks punch. Someone took out the alcohol. They took out the authority. Christ's version was hard liquor. Do as you would be done by. Why? Because He made you and this world, you and it are His, and He makes the rules. Because you will give an account. Because you will be judged as you judge others.

Authority, especially the authority of an infinite and holy Creator, whose words give us our very existence—that can give us morality.

Wait here. I'll bring back your bicycle.

If there are meta-beings, a god or gods who did not create the world, then they can tell us what to do the same way bullies can, though they have no jurisdiction. They can run our countries like Italian neighborhoods and along the same principles. Do it or get whacked. Bend your knees, slaughter bulls, lick dirt, give us your milk money. But might, even above the human level, does not make right.

But a creative God, a God without whom none of this would be, a God who spoke reality into being and shapes it even now, He has authority. This world is His. You are His the way my words are mine. We are dust spoken from nothing, shaped with the moisture of His breath, named and now-living.

St. Augustine: Love God and do as you please.

If you love Him, then you love holiness. What you please shouldn't present a problem.

◆

There are fairy shrimp in the deserts of southern Idaho. They were discovered just a few years ago by National Guardsmen in training.

For the first time in years, enough rain had fallen in the

desert to form puddles. In that very temporary world, strange white creatures were gliding, angels of puddle-death, devouring mosquito young and any other small swimming things. Four inches long, many-legged, Velcro-bellied to better store their prey, looking around their shallow world with mantis heads, these shrimp had lurked in dry, dormant eggs for a decade or more, somehow, at some point, laid in the desert.

I've given up on probabilities. They don't scare anyone. Why talk about the unlikelihood of any of this happening by accident? Any frog, any ladybug or butterfly is as unlikely as an Idaho desert shrimp, and yet there are millions of creatures chirping, crawling, and being formed from soup right now, relishing lives full of meaning, full of love and food and sunlight and mud—all gifts that trigger gratitude. And for gratitude to work, there must be one responsible—a Giver of gifts.

My wife sleeps beside me, even now, while I write. The earth has turned into shadow, though the moon-mirror is high, and the time has come for sane creatures to hold very still and think unintentional thoughts.

My love for her is more than the love a magnet has for a fridge. My love for her is driven by more than a quest to pass on my genes to equally worthless offspring. She and I have a story together. We are strings played together, a song and dance routine that we polish and practice every day. It is a love both hungry and fed, thirsty and always drinking. I look at her the way a girl looked at me from her wheelchair. I cannot hold myself back. I cannot stop repeating myself.

I will grant this much—it is a lot like an explosion, like a wave tumbling us up the beach to the place where our story will ripen like the summer grain, to the place where the Harvester will find us.

There is nothing accidental about the bright eyes my daughters use to see the world, or the sparks of joy that come to them as they discover small stories for the first time, stories of cats and squirrels, Winter and Spring, feasting and love and laughter, joy and gratitude.

When I lie on the ground, face down in the carpet, penitent with thankfulness for a life undeserved, for beauty and happiness unmerited, grateful for the stars and the starlings, for the grass and the leaves and the bound-up bales of love I've been given, I know what is coming. I can hear the voice of their mother egging them on.

Bone of my bone and flesh of my flesh.

Daughters on my back, kisses and laughter in my ears. A son's hands on my ankles, straining for the day when he can flip me easily. A smaller son, with few words to his tongue, grinding his young skull into mine, twisting and worming beneath my face. He needs no words. He looks up into my eyes, smiles, and slaps my cheek, picking a fight, waiting for his neck to be eaten. Waiting for laughter.

I stand, ripening in the sun, on a street corner by a coffee shop. The world spins on, undisturbed in its route. Summer has come with the loveliness of a mother. Heat, not warmth, now pours onto my face, aging me, taking me closer to death.

Let it. I am here to live my story, to love my story. I will not fail to savor any gift out of a desire for self-preservation. Self-preservation is not a great virtue in this story.

I have this world, and everything in it has me, poor trade though it is. I have a barbecue. I will use it tonight.

Over my shoulder a girl approaches, pushing a wheelchair. A man sits in it, twisted, drool dried on chapped lips beneath the tangles of an untrimmed moustache.

Nietzsche's voice is hard to understand. "The Christian concept of a god," he says. "The god as the patron of the sick, the god as a spinner of cobwebs, the god as a spirit—is one of the most corrupt concepts that has ever been set up in the world: it probably touches the low-water mark in the ebbing evolution of the god-type."

I want to ruffle his hair. I want to take the poor Lutheran boy's head in my hands and kiss his creased forehead. It is all I can do. I cannot set a bone, let alone a soul.

He moves on, preaching unbelief to an empty street.

And I move on, with the sun on my face. Clouds are growing in the west, glorious clouds piled up with rowdy care and sparked with electric life.

I fill my lungs with the world, with this life, with this gift beyond containing. There is only one thing I can say.

Thank you. And I must say it with my life. Through my life. To the end of my life.

And after.

THE PROBLEM OF KITTENS: CUTENESS AND BEAUTY

The air is thickening. It's not humid. This isn't that kind of heat. But the wind has died and the atmosphere is being compressed, pressurized, rubbing its socks in the carpet.

I am sweating down the lenses of my sunglasses, inside and out.

Locusts spent the morning crackling yellow wings around me, but now they are silent. While I climb my ladder into the eaves with my back to the south, the only motion comes from the yellow jackets and bald-faced hornets combing the wall, wondering where spit-crafted homes have gone, crushed behind new cedar siding.

The nail gun is hot enough to burn my hand. I can't leave it hooked on the ladder. It comes down with me and rests in the shade between cuts.

In the west there are clouds building, piling up toward the afternoon moon. They are the ones compressing this air. They are the ones creating an afternoon oppression so they can bring evening relief.

They are not cute, but they are beautiful.

There once was a rabbit named Marcus Aurelius. His story begins with him sitting at a farmers' market, a meat rabbit, intended for someone's pot.

He was priced at five dollars.

My aunt (to-be) purchased Marcus, but not for his meat. She bought him for friendship, for humor, for something warm and soft to hold. Marcus even knew how to wiggle his nose.

Have you ever heard a rabbit scream? They sound like pigs with a slightly higher pitch and more projection. The scream comes out in extreme duress, as a final prayer before the snake contracts, before the talons grip, before Mr. McGregor makes himself a stew.

The thing about Christians is that we usually want to pick one aspect of this world, one aspect of God's personality, and then stick with that.

Rabbits are soft and cuddle-puddly. Kittens are cute in baskets. Shall we latch on to an image of kittens, never growing, never hunting, never laying waste to small animal populations? Shall we stick with softness and warmth and long floppy ears and ignore the occasional scream in the bushes?

The story of Marcus Aurelius seemed to be all rainbows and joy. He was no longer a meat rabbit. His savior, my aunt, took him to befriend her kindergarteners, my older sister among them.

Marcus played with them at recess. He was brown and sleek and big and friendly.

Marcus grew fat.

In the summer after that glorious year in the kindergarten, when the fields had been baked and the country roads were warping the air with their heat, Marcus went to stay with some friends, farmers. Everyone knew he would like it there. Their house was set back in the fields where a rabbit should live, in a place where he could see the mountain.

My sister loved him. My aunt loved him. I, though my three-year-old mind retained nothing of it, must have loved him at the time.

The picture book of Marcus's life has a disturbing final page.

But such a promising beginning—spared from death, a friend to laughing five-year-olds, innocence and bliss.

Which is more beautiful—a sleek, shiny-eyed rabbit, well fed and well loved, named for a stoic philosopher-emperor, or a red-tailed hawk, sleek in a different way, floating on updrafting air cooked in the fields, with sharp eyes and pointy parts?

Marcus was taken into the yard to play. He loved playing with kids. It was all he'd ever known since that day in the farmers' market. He didn't know anything about hawks. No one had prepared him.

The hawk hit before anyone saw it dropping. Hawks tend to do that. But Marcus was fat, too heavy for the talons, too baggy and easily torn.

In the end, Marcus lay panting, mutilated in the yard. Witnesses were traumatized. The hawk, weary and hungrier than before, took itself back to the skies, no doubt looking for something smaller. Perhaps a kitten.

Marcus Aurelius met his end with as much dignity as a fat rabbit torn by beak and talon can.

I do not know where he was buried or if a stone now marks the place.

But he was never eaten.

Marcus Aurelius (fragmented from *Meditations*): Execute every act of thy life as though it were thy last.

Spoken like a dead Roman.

A tabby kitten lies on its back, looking at me out of upside-down eyes. This kitten has a message: "God hears even the smallest voice."

I could purchase this glossy 13.5" x 19" poster and hang it by my desk, right next to the Marine Disasters of Cape Cod.

Does the kitten believe what he's telling me? Will he feel guilt as he devours squirrels and voles and infant quail?

This work is changing my hands. They are blistering beneath calluses. The thick pads of skin are soft with sweat and heat. Once protections, now they slide around above fluid as I pull on the ladder rungs. I know what must happen. Over the next few days, when the blisters have drained, the calluses will be cast off and new ones will begin. I won't be able to build them back up before fall.

I'm ignoring the heat. Guzzling fluids when I measure and cut, swallowing and gasping, and then squinting at the spinning teeth as they blur through western cedar, rattling shards against my lenses.

My family is at the pool.

In one jarring second the blade sparks, the wood jerks in my hand. I release the trigger and step back to stare at my fingertip. A long splinter, two inches, sticks out from beneath the nail on my forefinger. It has burrowed in halfway to my cuticle. There is no blood, not yet. It's being held in by the western cedar.

I pull the splinter out and drop it on the ground along with the first drops of blood. The ants can drink it. They need the protein. Sweat is all they've been getting from me.

There is a poster, smaller than the other, but just as kittened. It has a yellow border, and is as perky as perky can be. The kitten seems slightly troubled. I look more closely. Oh, ho, I see it now!

The fuzzy puppy has the kitten's tail in its mouth. Don't worry. No kitten was hurt. It looks Photoshopped.

Message in bubbly font: "Help me to remember, Lord, nothing is going to happen today that you and I can't handle together."

As long as nothing bigger than a puppy happens.

The air moves. Something rumbles in the distance—a truck straining at its trailer? The air-conditioning on the hospital roof carried by this first afternoon breeze?

Or thunder. The sky's whips are cracking somewhere in Washington State. Weeds are tumbling and the wind is shaping dust into devils to play in the fields, small cousins to the big funnels that wade through Midwestern skies.

I finish my cut and walk to the ladder, sucking on my finger.

Two red-tailed hawks float high above me. They live here now, in this neighborhood, nested high in a blue spruce. I wonder what they find to eat. Kittens? Pet rabbits? I wonder how clearly their eyes can see the gathering storm and when they will take to their nest, a home stationed in the highest point on this block.

How many hawks die from lightning strikes?

How would I know? I climb my metal ladder. At the top, a cluster of yellow jackets are swarming on a rung. Balancing with siding on one shoulder, I reach into my bags for the death I purchased yesterday. It is black and full of aerosol.

"Today is your death day," I say out loud. "You have lived full lives and ruined many picnics, scared many children and eaten your fill of watermelon. Or maybe you haven't. Either way . . ."

They convulse and drop out of the sky. I watch them for a moment, where they squirm beside the foundation. Today's count is over fifty.

If my finger didn't hurt, if I wasn't losing my favorite calluses, if my son hadn't been stung so many times this summer, then maybe they would have lived. But not likely.

Why do Christians think of purity, holiness, and even divinity as something with big eyes and soft fur? Why do we so often ignore the beautiful in exchange for the cute?

What should I learn about God from kittens and puppies? He made them; certainly they can teach me something. He made rabbits, too, and took softness to new levels when He worked on their fur. And then He gave them teeth that can curl like corkscrews . . . and that scream.

And on the sixth day, He made the naked mole rats. And they were good.

Naked mole rats are not cute (or beautiful in the normal way). They live in colonies (a sort of mammalian social insect) and function with a queen, an extra long queen, adapted to both navigate tunnels and carry the next generation of blind, naked, toothy workers. The queen will carry up to five litters per year, and each litter can run an average of twelve (and up to twenty-seven) pups.

Thanks to the intrepid photographic efforts of people I don't know, I have seen footage of a queen mole rat lying in her chamber, her noble king at her kicking, squirming, translucent side. The mole rats are formed in an active, tunneled womb. Life in the "hive" is spacious.

Can we get that straining queen onto a poster, please? Can I distribute that image to the women of Christendom?

God hears even the smallest voices, yea, even the voice of the unborn naked mole rat.

I'm seeing a yellow border. Pick your own font.

The winds are His messengers. Angelos, angel, messenger. Evangel.

I have moved my ladder. The wind is growing. Siding has patched its way further up the house. I know I am racing something much bigger and faster than I am. The wind itself makes my racing easier. The sweat is carried away. The pressurized heat has been pushed further east, where some farmer can now pull off his stained hat and wipe his brow in the stillness.

The hawks are out of the sky.

No doubt my family is out of the pool.

What is this message the wind is carrying? What is the moral? Would someone type it on a card for me?

At the top of my ladder, when I can see above the neighbor's trees, the message is clearer.

There will be hail, or rain in fat well-fed drops. I can see it frozen in its diagonal fall. From this distance it looks only like an artist licked His thumb and smudged the cloud earthward. It looks frozen, inspirational-postcard-ready. When I am standing inside the storm, the message will be clearer. Impressionism will travel on. Realism comes in its wake.

Realism. I have an angelic blessing. At least I think that's what this is. It's a card with a picture of a soft, puffy-dressed, aproned woman. She's been done with thin lines and gentle water colors.

The woman's dress is purple with flowers. Her hair is permed and her apron is broad and white, covering the expanse of her torso. The apron has a cursive word on it, drawn to look like embroidery.

Faith.

The poor woman also has cankles in the extreme, and slippers decorated with lopsided, stitched-on stars. Even weirder is her face. She has no mouth or nose, simply an oval pleasantness (she's white) with two dot eyes and large pink circles on her cheeks from all those angelic kisses she's been getting. Either that, or she's insecure about a total absence of facial features and hits the blush a little hard to compensate.

She has wings, and I'm glad for her, given the ankle situation.

Angel, angel, what's your message?

Right. No mouth. But there's some writing on the corner of the card.

Be joyful in hope, patient in affliction, faithful in prayer.

Paul wrote those words to the Christians in Rome. He wrote those words to Christians in a city where men and women and children had been fed to big cats, once kittens, in front of sell-out crowds. In Rome, Christians were tied to stakes and burned in order to provide patio lighting for Nero's dinner orgies. In Rome, Christians had been forced to worship in tunneled tombs, shelves lined with skulls. No better than the mole rats, they worshipped in small death chambers filled with the life of word and sacrament.

This is the first world. We need such reminders delivered by cankled grandmothers, pinned to the fridge with little fishy magnets.

In other places in the world, Christians died today and died for their baptisms.

Should we send these angels to Sudan? Should we send them to Indonesia and Iran, Korea and China? Are the winged grandmothers available with their embroidered aprons?

Ezekiel: Behold, a whirlwind came out of the north, a great cloud, and a fire infolding itself, and a brightness was about it, and out of the midst thereof as the colour of amber, out of the midst of the fire. Also out of the midst thereof came the likeness of four living creatures. And this was their appearance; they had the likeness of a man. And every one had four faces, and every one had four wings. And their feet were straight feet; and the sole of their feet was like the sole of a calf's foot: and they sparkled like the colour of burnished brass. And they had the hands of a man under their wings on their four sides; and they four had their faces and their wings. Their wings were joined one to another; they turned not when they went; they went every one straight forward. As for the likeness of their faces, they four had the face of a man, and the face of a lion, on the right side: and they four had the face of an ox on the left side; they four also had the face of an eagle. Thus were their faces: and their wings were stretched upward; two wings of every one were joined one to another, and two covered their bodies.

Holiness is terrible. It comes with the whirlwind. It is a purifying fire. We are not the first Christians to trivialize the cherubim. We are not the first to make things soft on our imaginations and comfortable in our dreams.

When you think of a cherub, do you see a gingham dress full of grandma? Do you see a fat, winged infant peeing in a fountain? Do you see something riding on the wings of a storm, something at home in the funnel clouds? Something with four faces and four wings, the color of burnished brass, unconsumed by an infolding fire?

The trite is more comfortable. I like angels I can hug. Forget the pillar of fire; a teddy bear is a more fitting icon of holiness.

Do you think that your hands will not blister in Heaven? Or do you think that you will look on your blisters differently? Do you think that your body, that flesh that now holds you back, will finally be put away and you will be free to listen to an eternal concert from the comfort of an ethereal massage chair? And thank goodness, since the music will be classical and sleep will be your only defense.

Will you have a harp and sit on a cloud?

You will be given a new body, a better body, a body that won't break down or decay under its labor. This body that houses you now, it is but a vapor to the flesh that waits for you.

When Christ rose, He rose in the flesh. He was no ghost, and yet He walked through walls. The walls were the ghosts, and so are we. We are children when it comes to labor, when it comes to love, when it comes to shaping this world.

The wind is building, but my ladder is heavy, and the rain hasn't yet found this corner of the world. Bricks and a tarp sit beside my tools.

At the top of my ladder, it is hard for me to work when I cannot take my eyes off the sky. I want to climb down and extend this ladder to its final rung. I want to climb onto my roof and stand on the peak, welcoming the wind.

I climb, filling my nostrils with the smell of ozone dragged down from its heights. This smell is the glory of the storm. The trees bend before it. The rain hits hot streets, finds dusty asphalt and gives off its own aroma, an offering.

In a summer storm, it is hard to find a place that smells holier than a parking lot.

If I met with an angel, I wouldn't ask it for a cookie. If I had eyes to see what Ezekiel saw, I would need to be lifted off my face. I would need to be reminded that I looked at a fellow creature, at a creature now ruled by Man. The Man.

I am too small and in the wrong body for such open eyes. The wind is enough to overwhelm me. The shaking trees capture how I feel, bowing and breaking as the sky rushes by.

◆

God invented skunks.

Fat and nasty, the woodland punks have no concept of their size, nor do they need to. They will do their handstands and obscenely march toward any predator—facing grizzlies down with nothing more than inappropriate glandular behavior.

Skunks wander through town at night, chowing on smaller cats. Lonely people put flyers on telephone poles, but the rest of us aren't sad. Every cat has it coming.

But so does every skunk.

God also invented owls, gave them hearing as sharp as their eyes and near silent flight. He neglected to give many of them any notable sense of smell.

A skunk need not fear a cougar or a grizzly, an entire pack of wolves, or the wiliest coyote.

But while he is busying himself in your yard, polishing the bones of your cat, he is as vulnerable as Marcus Aurelius, the onetime meat rabbit.

His back arching and odor spritzing will do nothing against one of the flat-faced, feathered night-killers.

God hears even the smallest voices, and an owl's young are fed while I shut my windows against the twilight smell.

Painter, Painter, paint me a picture of what God is like, and of the secret, happy places where He would love to take me.

Would you like a gilt frame? (The charge is minimal.)

I see waterfalls, little gentle ones, with room temperature water so I won't feel much if I dip my toes. I see round pink bushes and blue ones and white ones. They must smell lovely. I'm sure no white crab spiders lurk in the blooms. I'm sure there aren't any thorns.

Oh, but there will be rabbits. Lots of rabbits, curled up in sleeping bundles beneath the thornless roses.

Will they eat the roses?

Eat? They won't eat anything. If they ate, they'd have to, you know, poo. This is Heaven. We won't have bodies that need food in Heaven, and neither will the rabbits. I doubt we'll even have sharp objects. Safety scissors for all the saints! Stick tennis balls on every Rocky Mountain peak. We wouldn't want the angels to snag their aprons delivering the snickerdoodles.

Christianity is no longer about changing the world. Christianity is no longer about facing the darkness and walking into shadow with souls full of light. We don't see evil as a thing to be conquered, we don't see life as a story with any kind of arc. We don't want our God to be the God of falcons and mole rats and skunk justice.

This God you worship invented rabbits. But this is also the God of your lower intestine (a design He was rather pleased with). This is the God who invented sex, and not as some sort of pornographic waxy-bodied, two-dimensional abstraction. This God invented everything that comes along with sex between a real man and a real woman.

This God made sex a destroyer and made men to sing "House of the Rising Sun" and write *Anna Karenina*. This God made it a gift and set it in a walled garden (privately owned, no tours, no public subsidies).

This God invented moss and centipedes and bats and giant centipedes that dangle from cave roofs and eat bats. This God invented sunlight and atmospheres and a rotating world to catch the light and sprawl color through the skies. This God invented forest fires in Montana. Millions of acres burn, and where I sit, to the west of the flames, the smoke boosts the sunset into total domination of the sky. This God invented Christians to take pictures of those sunsets, built with flames and hot summer death, and put them on postcards along with the slogan "I come to the garden alone."

This God invented armpits. Does He grieve when they make you stink?

This God invented leeches and mosquitoes and bedbugs that bite. Did He not? Then who did? What are they made of? Is God trying to rid the world of such cooties but hasn't been a quick enough study at the art of pest control?

Why do these things not fit on our postcards? Why do we omit them in the abridged extra-holy version of reality for families?

They are here. They are words. What do they tell us? What is their role in the story?

The apostle Paul: All flesh is seed, awaiting resurrection.

C. S. Lewis: Animals are flesh. They will march into the sun of new life.

People: Ha. What will you do with the mosquitoes? Will good ones go to Heaven?

C. S. Lewis: If the worst came to the worst, a Heaven for mosquitoes and a Hell for people could very conveniently be combined.

Don't put that in the brochure.

Heaven will be wonderful (understatement). It will be more wonderful than we can imagine, even if our imaginations weren't so stunted by marshmallow visions. You will have a body more physical than this one. Heaven will be hard and bright, and the winds will be strong. You will have the body and the eyes and the purified, well-aged soul to bear it.

We will remake this world with blistered hands.

Do not resent your place in the story. Do not imagine yourself elsewhere. Do not close your eyes and picture a world without thorns, without shadows, without hawks. Change this world. Use your body like a tool meant to be used up, discarded, and replaced. Better every life you touch. We will reach the final chapter. When we have eyes that can stare into the sun, eyes that only squint for the Shekinah, then we will see laughing children pulling cobras by their tails, and hawks and rabbits playing tag.

But we cannot hope to reach the final chapter by dreaming, by holding our collective breath and staring at unshaded acrylic escape paintings. The only road to that final chapter began at the garden and led into the wilderness. It runs through these chapters. Live now. Relish the tensions, the challenges, and laugh at the petty pains.

In the Passover, in the old way, the house was to be purified, every yeast germ removed. Long codes of purification were handed out to characters then, characters in those early chapters. Shellfish tainted you. Polyester tainted you. Foreskins tainted you. Human holiness was fragile in those days.

Things have changed. A great sheet was lowered in Peter's dream. Eat. Have sushi. Try a snake. Prawns are a treat wrapped in bacon with a spicy barbecue sauce.

Food is holy when you eat it, when it is used to strengthen a body used to strengthen the world.

Leave the yeast. Be the yeast. Do not fear the shadowy places. You will never be the first one there. Another went ahead and down until He came out the other side.

The problem of evil brings its own strength. We do not need to strengthen it more by imagining perfection to be cross-stitch and cookies and uneaten, uneating kittens.

The world is already more wonderful than we can imagine. Heaven will be better still.

I do not doubt that whatever gates there may be, they will be pearly. But I know how pearls are made. Do you?

In Heaven, the gates will be made of oyster spit.

Exercise: Envision those oysters.

Painter, Painter, paint me some light. Paint me a village far from pain. Paint me lush hedges and glowing windows and puddles that shine.

Such scenes exist, like rabbits, like raindrops on roses and whiskers on kittens, bright copper kettles and warm woolen mittens.

Painter, Painter, find the other shoe. Drop it.

Everything has its place in this frame. Everything has its position on the stage. The world is full of comfortable things. The world is full of soft beauty and gentle lapping waves. We would be fools to ignore the gentleness and get caught up in the grit, only able to tell dark stories. But a world of gentle touches is no truer than a world gone black. Put the colors in their places. Paint a true picture, with tension.

After every rain, look at your feet. As the sun sets, admire the freshness of the world and how tasteful it looks with that golden tint. Look at the pale, bloated carnage.

Every glowing puddle is filled with the earthworm dead. Why they come to such moist ends I do not know. Are they called by name when their earthly tour is over, or do they simply love the water without knowing how to swim?

These are the puddle lemmings. In the summer rains, they die; they suicide by the thousands.

Realism is not puffy-faced angels and realism is not grit standing alone. One school, made up of aunts and grandmothers and people pleasant and soft to hug, focuses on angel pillows and paintings that are all pastels and gold bits. The other school, the school desperate for a faith and a story with an edge, focuses on anything that belongs in a bathroom stall. Novels should go from gray to black to a glimmer of gray. Incest, abuse, rubber-banded forearms, black eyeliner, and abandonment—these things are real. Happiness isn't real. Joy isn't real, especially not joy in hardship. Resentment is real. A life of bitterness is real.

Rabbits suck (unless I feed them to my python), but kittens are cool—because they are fuzzy killers, ironic paradox.

The Problem Part One: Cute things exist, and they are objectively cute. The movie isn't over. I'm sorry to tell you this, but the world will end happily. Sorrow goes down in a barrage of bullets, and Grief is executed after a fair trial. Eyelashes exist, and my daughters' are curly. They love to brush them on my cheeks, and that fleeting touch, that dragging whisper, is more real than your heroin dreams. It is a better picture of the World and History than all your whining.

When Hitler has been forgotten and Stalin is the name of a new brand of bubblegum, butterfly kisses will live on.

The Problem Part Two: The world is rated R, and no one is checking IDs. Do not try to make it G by imagining the shadows away. Do not try to hide your children from the world forever, but do not pretend there is no danger. Train them. Give them sharp eyes and bellies full of laughter. Make them dangerous. Make them yeast, and when they've grown, they will pollute the shadows.

Keep the angel pillows if you like. They will not taint you. You can rest your head on them while you watch the summer sun set—a bloody sun bathing in a smoky sky.

The sky above my eaves is still blue, still bright with the hot afternoon. But the pearly gates have filled the west and are overflowing.

Wind is racing now, sliding beneath my ladder, dividing through the bushes and chasing dust down the alley.

Cherubim are coming. I can hear their laughter, the roaring in the sky.

My ladder slides, only an inch, but enough to make me jerk.

Now is the time to get down. Now is the time for rabbits to find their bushes.

The first hailstones bounce in the grass beneath me and rattle off the ladder.

I do not want to lose my flesh. I want better flesh. I want to be able to run with these horses, like Elijah.

Has anyone known joy like Elijah racing the storm?

These cherubim are not destroyers, though they have destroyed. This hail is not falling on Egypt.

When I stand at the top of a cliff, I have no fear of falling accidentally. I fear that I will jump. This wind speaks to the clay of my body. This wind, this breath of God is what first filled Adam's lungs and gave him life.

The clouds are dark. The yellow jackets have hidden. Hail falls faster. I cannot shake a can and spray against its sting.

Now is the time to get down, to get away from this ladder. I am a fat rabbit.

On the ground I am not yet ready to tarp my tools. I am waiting. I have been waiting all day.

The sky splits and the ground quivers beneath me. The reflection of the world wobbles in my windows, shaken by the burnished brass drums of cherubim, come with an infolding fire.

Ozone. The smell sates my need, and I hurry to my tools.

There was once a rabbit never kept in a hutch and never sold for five dollars. This rabbit was fast, and he did not fear the open places. He did not fear the falcons.

I have watched this rabbit run, over and over again, replaying tape captured by a lucky soul, witness to a strange reversal.

In a dive, the fastest of the falcons has been clocked at well over two hundred miles per hour.

At first, streaking dust, with death floating on its heels, the rabbit outraces the falcon on a straight track. The raptor pulls up and circles, giving its prey more respect in the next dive. The prey adjusts as well, veering at the last of all possible moments, brushing bodies with the hunter as the bird piles into the dust. Again the falcon circles; again the rabbit takes no cover.

The rabbit runs, the bird dives, coming at this daredevil from the front, head to head with odd long-eared confidence.

The rabbit does not veer again. He does not flinch. As the

falcon swoops toward it, the rabbit leaps, skimming the feathered back, kicking off, boosting its own flight.

And so the story ends.

For now. Until some unseen page brings the death of that flesh, the end of that body so well used.

My tarp needs extra bricks after I've laid my ladder on the ground.

I am running now, pounded by rain, by cast-off drops from this ocean in the sky.

Wind is painting my shirt to my chest. Branches lie in the street.

I hear sirens, shrill complaints against the cherubim.

I hear a small voice. I look up. My beautiful three-year-old, curly-haired, already pool-wet before the rain, is shivering in a towel. I hear her mother calling.

I scoop her up and try to hold her close, but she pulls her head away, squinting at the storm, rain running off her eyelashes.

We are on the porch. We have reached the front door.

She speaks wisdom like an oracle, shrugging, laughing.

"God loves noise."

Out of the mouths of babes.

I smile.

The cherubim beat their drums, messengers carrying water to Montana.

SUMMER HIATUS: SAND CASTLES

I am good with a bucket. I will defeat the ocean.

The goal is not detail. I don't want a sand castle with gothic lines and toothpick-etched windows. I want something big enough to sit in. A foxhole. And I won't retreat up to the safe sand, well above the highest tide. I will carve out my legacy here, straddling the wash point where the foam sizzles and the sand crabs burrow. I will do it while the tide rises. And the tide is always rising. Every day it rocks back on its heel to build momentum, to get another run; every day it crawls, slipping, up the beach.

The ocean can never forget the Flood. It has tasted mountains. Waking and sleeping, it chews.

I dig trenches, canals, drainage points, and pile up U-shaped dikes that I can afford to lose. Let them go. They are quickly replaced. For now, they break the foam-blow and send the wash around the foxhole.

My son is unappreciative. The prodigal. He digs for sand crabs. He even finds them. A daughter sits up high on the beach beside her mother. She likes sand. Dry sand. And she ignores the ocean. The youngest, thick and unintimidated, likes hugging dogs and grabbing cats. She is always walking, happy, toward the water. She will not be distracted by a sand stronghold, or crabs, or trucks and shovels. She wants only to pet the breakers.

I am alone, building this inheritance, this sand bench inside a foxhole. They would rather eat with pigs.

My wife wants me to chase children. But the waves will not wait.

Not far from here, there is a house on an island that was once a peninsula. Beside it, the bones of a lighthouse lie bare, like the ribs of a whale. The house, shattered and hollow, has been inherited by elephant seals, and they will keep it until the ocean robs even them.

I will be washed away. I will be battered and picked at. I will stoop and sag. My skin will be stretched and folded and eventually pounded into sand. Decay will catch me. But for now, until the day I lose, I will win. I will pack my body's walls with strength it cannot keep. I will eat and drink. And when the tide is out, rocking back, I will close my eyes and rest my bones.

If I had Quick Crete, I would use it. Who could stop me?

Lifeguards? I don't see any, and if they're around, they're probably more worried about people drowning than they are about concrete-laced castles.

But even the quickest of concretes couldn't help me. The ocean wouldn't care. A couple hundred stiffening pounds would mean nothing to it. I could park my truck here and it would be gone in the morning. The waves might just bend it in half and leave it hanging on the cliff. Or, if they were in the right mood, they could pull it out to the kelp beds and give it to a needy family of leopard sharks.

One time, I did leave a mark on this beach. A dent beside a rock. The rock was connected to a spur, and the spur, buried beneath the sand, to the cliff. I dug my foxhole beside it, canalled and diked, and diligently maintained. In the morning, the sand was dimpled where I'd labored.

And I was proud.

My daughters are too small to sit in this gift to them. I grab two older nieces and my son. The three, safe behind sand walls, laugh and taunt the ocean. The foam breaks on the outer dike and wraps around my creation. The walls hold. The children yell. The water rolls away.

The three are bouncing, waiting. They want another one. They want destruction.

So do I.

I will beat the ocean, but only by being beaten. I've lived inside sand walls—we all do—and they are always torn away.

Generations, people, black and white ancestors with forgotten names and forgotten graves, have broken the waves and been broken.

Not long ago, a woman I loved called to me at church.

"I wanted to show you," she said. "I knew you'd like this." She lifted her hat, and I saw the head the doctors had shaved and the curving line where they'd split her skull. I hugged her. I smelled her, treasuring up all that I could of that grandmotherly body with the life still in. She said good-bye and kissed my cheek. She'd already picked her box. She, I will see again. Those lips, never.

The waves come. They tear through the walls and erase the dikes. The three children jump up and run, falling with laughter.

This is how it is. It is my turn to be the wall, to lie down and break the foam. I will dig and scrape and yell and curse the ocean. But I want those waves to come while the children laugh. And when they grind my sand, I will leave more than a dimple behind me. I will leave others, laughing others, impatient for their turn to be the wall.

They are good with buckets. They will defeat the ocean.

HELL: THE FINAL CONVERSATION

Fall—ripen, blaze, fade.

On my side of the street, the sidewalk is a tunnel, a path through age. I stand in it every day. On one edge, the dark basalt wall runs the length of the block. On the other, maple trees stand in their long row, arms uplifted, tired arms stretching over the path, in places even fingering the sloping earth held back by the wall.

Those fingers are yellowing. Somehow, they know that our spinning world has reached the Autumn corner of our orbit. They know because they taste the light, because they smell it, because they look up at the sun and see its back. They feel the world leaning away as we bank into the curve.

Let us grow old, they say. Let us sweeten the air with rot. Let us die.

I stop for a second, for a minute or ten, and feel this place. I watch this glorious fade-out, the beginning of a death, a death celebrated with flaming confetti.

The very first leaves are falling, eager to begin. Thousands more hang on, savoring life well aged and air that smells like football.

When I grow old, I will wear these colors and change my name to Fall. I will not sweeten the air. People will not stop on the street to marvel at how the sun passes through my fingers. But that will not keep me from dying.

Every year, fifty-five million people die. Six thousand die every hour of every day (one hundred every minute). This is according to the flyer hung on my doorknob yesterday morning.

I do not know if the numbers are accurate. I do not need to know; the spirit is certainly true. If you have skin and bones, if you have breath, someday you will lose it all.

The flyer asks me a question in bold: Are you prepared?

For good measure, clip art of a many-tooled pocketknife lingers in the margin.

I scan the front. I scan the back. There is no direct mention of Hell. But the words *judge* and *judgment* both appear. So does "spiritual death."

If God is good, if He is the God of small, fuzzy animals, if He is the God of summer thunderstorms, then why would He throw me into Hell? I happen to be much better company than most people I know. Why would I burn eternally for nothing worse than occasionally fudging my sales reports?

Worse, why would He burn me when I've worked in soup kitchens, when I donate the occasional dollar to the American Heart Association, when I weep over school shootings and hurricanes?

Not long ago, an old man was dying. All old men die, but this one was different, because I loved him. He was grandfather to my wife, and my children share his blood.

My wife traveled to him, where he waited for Death in Arizona. She took a fresh-faced daughter, born in the fall, in the Spring of her own life. She took round, sunlit eyes into the shadow.

He was dying of not wanting to live. He was dying of refusing to eat.

St. Augustine described Hell as a place with both pains of sense (physical) and pains of loss, resulting from simple separation from God.

Thomas Aquinas echoed him, but with perhaps more relish for physical specifics.

Theologians like Kvanvig prefer to think of Hell as a place where the torment is purely one of separation from the goodness of God. Hell is existential pain.

C. S. Lewis, in *The Great Divorce*, placed Hell in a very small crack in the ground of Heaven.

From a sermon preached by John Donne, poet: "When all is done, the hell of hells, the torment of torments, is the everlasting absence of God . . . . to fall out of the hands of the living God, is a horror beyond our expression, beyond our imagination."

I am inclined to capitalize the word Hell, because I think of it as a place. Like Topeka.

Jean-Paul Sartre, in his play *No Exit*: Hell is other people.

A writer for *Wired* modified that slightly: Hell is other people's music.

The two can be conveniently combined.

I am not Enoch. I will not skip steps and be caught directly up into Heaven. My route will take me through the mud. I am not Elijah, and there will be no fiery chariot. I am not Arthur. No mythology will spring up around stories of my return. I am not Moses. My body will not be so sacred that the archangel and Lucifer will struggle over the abandoned flesh.

I will turn slowly to dust in a box. Or, if I go with a hip wicker-woven casket, I will quickly become compost. These eyes, this mind, my divoted shin, this tongue—let them feed the sod. I will be elsewhere.

Have you ever seen the shriveled back of a bean or the dried husk of a sunflower seed clinging to the stalk of a tall living plant, a reminder of origins, of a death that brought new green life?

Some seeds were thrown among the thorns, others on shallow ground, and still others on stones.

Those seeds will never climb into the sky, clinging to a fresh green back.

There once was a man, a thief, sentenced to death by the justices of Rome.

What was his role? We only know of one purpose that he ever served. We do not know if he ever had children or what became of them if he did. We do not know if he ever beat his wife or thought of himself as noble.

What we know is that soldiers held him down while he screamed. We know that men with mallets drove rough iron spikes through his wrists and feet, splaying him against heavy lumber.

He was in the big scene. He was born and raised and walked to a death at the climax of history. He was one of two to die beside the Messiah, to be there bleeding with Him, looking on the naked form of a dying God.

The other died well, and no man has ever died in better company or with better words shaped by sinful lips. He was with the Son in the final moments of His first flesh, and he walked through the veil with Him. He bled when the earth shook, when the Holy of Holies was ripped open to the nations, to the unclean. He was there when the role of yeast changed, and unlike the pious disciples shedding tears at the feet of those three crosses, he traveled on with his Maker.

Christ to the apostle Peter: Where I am going, you cannot follow.

Christ to the thief: Come with me. We die together, a thief and the Maker of the world. Walk with the Infinite made flesh into the belly of the whale. Stand close while reality quakes. Watch while Death is taken by the throat. Today you will be with me in Paradise.

Stories don't end at death.

The other thief, bleeding, gasping, suffocating under the pressure of crucifixion, chose different last words. With his final breaths, from one cross to another, from one body breaking under its own weight, to a Body breaking under the weight of the world, he mocked the Messiah.

What was done with *him*? Where is he now?

The leaves are not falling. Not yet. They are changing, growing, accepting a new role. When they do fall, I shall rake them. I will scrape this sidewalk until the cast-off many-colored robes are mounded high. Then I will heave them into my yard. I will watch my sweatered children discover and rediscover the joy of playing in death, the joy of jumping, laughing, sneezing, and rolling in the remnants of another year, the joy of being buried and resurrected, of climbing in and out of a grave.

Do not mourn the leaves.

I remember climbing on my father. I remember the sensation of his ribs beneath my feet. That time is fresh in imagination, but it is gone.

Now I drop to the floor, and I hear the cry go up among greener leaves.

A pile. A pile. Knees and feet find my back and try to balance while I roll. Bodies tumble, laughing. I am wearing an oversized sweatshirt, and someone is worming beneath it.

A daughter's face emerges from my chest, smiling beneath my chin.

"I cannot stay here forever," she says simply, with her eyebrows high. She is wise.

I smile. "Why not?"

"Because I will grow. I will be too big and you will be old and sparkly."

"Sparkly?"

"Yes. And then you will die."

I laugh. She remains serious.

"And then I will get old and sparkly and I will die, and my children will put me in the ground."

I wrap my arms tight around her tiny body, suddenly aching, pressing her life as close to mine as I can. Bone of my bone. She slithers back beneath the thick cloth, back out of the pile of leaves. There is no sadness on her face, none in her voice. Why would there be? She jumps and spins, slipping on a plastic cow.

"We will be in Heaven," she says, bouncing on her bare

toes. But now her brow furrows. Wrongness has found her. "Where is my balloon?" she asks.

Do not mourn the leaves.

I wrote a letter for Grandpa Marty. My wife took it with her as she hurried through the skies; she took it into the house, into the room chosen for his death, and sat with it beside his bed.

He was a writer, a man with eyes and ears for story. He was choosing his end, choosing his final chapter. He wanted consciousness to be done. In *his* book, flesh was all he had, flesh was all there was. He would simply cease to be. The chemical reaction that had been his mind would stop. The chemicals, the sum of the man, would fragment and find new homes.

I wrote him as a critic. I disliked the ending—a bad one can sour and ruin even a well-crafted novel, a good one can recast the pallor of a lifetime. I asked him to consider changing those back pages.

Where is the final triumph, the final laughter, the final twist?

My wife read the letter to him while he licked dry, cracking lips, and he took it from her. I have it now. In pen, wobbling up the side, he wrote his first reply in caps—an expletive.

Then he asked her to read it again.

Louis the XV was as debauched a man as ever helped cause a peasant revolution. With a taste for virgins (supplied by his more official mistress), he is alleged to have said a prayer of thanksgiving for an absence of venereal disease before each tryst—rumors of far more vicious and exuberant behavior were constant among the French people.

Louis, as he yellowed, as his stem weakened and he fell from the tree: "I have been a great sinner, doubtless, but I have ever observed Lent with a most scrupulous exactness. I have caused more than a hundred thousand masses to be said for the repose of unhappy souls, so that I flatter myself I have not been a very bad Christian."

Sun king, where are you now?

Knowing he had reached the end, William Blake died trying to sketch his wife on their forty-fifth anniversary.

Blake: "I cannot think of death as more than the going out of one room into another."

Oscar Wilde: "I am dying, as I have lived, beyond my means."

Most Christians, apart from philosophical discussions, are less than inclined to bring up the subject of Hell. Even people with a desire to hang things on my doorknob would rather say that I am "under God's judgment," and I don't blame them. Hellfire and damnation preachers left deep, nervous scars on the psyches of evangelists.

No one wants to judge.

No one with any social instincts wants to proclaim

damnation. No one wants to talk about fire. Dante's age is gone, an age of vivid hellish tours, with even popes pictured in the Inferno, inverted, eternal flames dancing on the arches of their feet.

But if Hell (of any sort) exists, if souls will find themselves in a house of lamentation or a house of joy, if pain and agony wait for them, should we shuffle our feet nervously and hope they don't ask pointed questions, hope they don't request a judgment?

◆

The memory is only partial. The old pub was generous on week-nights between the hours of five and seven. Free food found its way magically onto a wheeled cart, and drafts of onsite brews were two dollars a pull.

It was a haven for poor, ungrateful graduate students. Free mozzarella sticks were mocked. Shepherd's pie was demanded by right (it had been given once). Hot wings were considered minimal. Didn't they realize that this was our evening meal?

We sat around a table, nursing two dollars in liquid form and eating free cheese. My Catholic friend was talking about professors. An atheist was complaining about parking. Another atheist, a girl, was sitting thoughtfully, staring at us, at the "believers" outed in various seminar discussions.

When the conversation lagged, she asked her question.

"Do you think I'm going to Hell?"

"Yes," my Catholic friend said without hesitation. He looked around. "I do."

People laughed, not because it was a joke, but because he was serious and unembarrassed. He was never embarrassed—an attribute I admired.

She looked at me and leaned forward, waiting for the Protestant version.

"I don't know," I said. "Don't you want to?"

"What do you mean?" she made an excellent questioning face—cocked head and eyebrows behind glasses. It was perfect for the classroom. "Why would I want to go to Hell?"

"God is who He is. Do you *want* to be with Him?"

Hell is voluntary. Would you like to go?

Grandpa Marty heard the letter many times. He asked to keep it with him. He had it beside him when he slipped into his coma—a sleep that only grew deeper until finally, even his thoughts stopped and the strands that wove soul to body, long tattered, frayed to a finish.

Stand by the freshly dead. Look down at the body confused, grieved. But they are still a being. They are not only a chemical reaction that you have watched collapse, a reaction that has shifted from the maintenance of cells and the extraction and distribution of energy, to the breaking down of cells, rot and decomposition.

You look down at the body, at that pile of leaves, but the person is no longer there. The leaves have fallen.

Mourn the tree.

I do not pretend to know what manner of Hell waits on those who do not desire God. And it will be a question of desire, not belief. Dislike, not disbelief. The dead will stand before Him, still living in another way. There will be no ignorance then. There will be no confusion, no distant uneducated native (used in evangelical guilt trips) who never heard the good news and is surprised to find himself beneath an eternal ax. All will believe in God in the end, and all will be justly judged by the standard they themselves used to judge others.

Even the demons believe. The demons saw the cross. The demons remember Easter.

Heaven or Hell is about love and hate. Do you love God or do you hate Him? Is He foul in your nostrils? Do you see His art and wish your arm was long enough to reach His face? Do you spit and curse like Nietzsche? Would you trade places with the damned thief so that you might see Him die and know that God Himself heard your challenges?

Then Hell is for you. Hell is for you because God is kind and reserves a place for those who loathe Him to the end, an eternal exile, a joyless haven for those who would eternally add to their guilt, a place where blasphemy will be new every morning. A place less painful and less terrible than the alternative.

Unless you change, Heaven, the Shekinah, the close presence of that burning Holiness, the presence of the creator God and the face of the exalted Word, the winds and fire of that storm of joy would be a worse hell than Hell itself, a worse burning than any figurative (or literal) flames.

In the end, there will be no escaping Hell, because all else will be Heaven. There will be no need for walls or chains or any kind of cell, because Hell will be that place farthest away from His smell. A place you will hate but have no desire to leave. Earth, every corner of it, will no longer be neutral.

Hell will be hell. Now His grace is all around us. Believer and unbeliever both warm their faces in the sun, both watch the leaves repaint themselves, both see the stars at night.

If you love Him, then look to His Son to change you. Look to Him for eyes hard enough to pierce the cherubim games, for unbursting ears to hear the planets sing, for feet to anchor you in the ocean's laughing, pounding mountains—wet offerings to a Master.

Look to Him for a heart capable of loving Him.
The fires will burn hotter in Heaven.
Our tongues will learn their taste.

If you displease Him, He will displease you. He will put you away and remove the grace you have experienced in this world. With the crutches of His goodness gone, He will leave people to themselves, leave them to their own corrupt desires and devices.

Have you seen people left to themselves? Did you complain about the absence of God when you did? Where is He in the genocides? Where is He among the gunned-down and maimed?

You have glimpsed Hell, a place where God allows that which displeases Him. A place where people will live in shadow. All of those shadows will be overthrown as the Son rises. All the darkness will be pushed and shoveled and trampled, and then swept into a corner, a crack in the ground.

You may live there if you like. Even in the final chapter, contrast will exist. A shadow will remain to set off the blazing elsewhere.

You have nothing in and of yourself. You and I are made of clay and spit. Any holiness of ours is polluted beyond our petty comprehension.

I have nothing to offer Him but a bent neck, a neck He helped me bend. I have nothing to offer Him but filth, and He has taken it. He exchanged it for blood like wine, and His own body broken like bread.

Do you resent this world, this art? Do you hate Him for cancer, for car wrecks, and for the sudden shocking sleep of the young? Do you hate Him for those waves that break too high, for those hours when far more than six thousand die? Do you resent your story? Your height, your baldness, your itchy feet and unstable lower intestine, the forest fire sunsets and your own mortality?

Buy cream for your wrinkles. Whiten your teeth. Have doctors staple back your scalp until you die and decompose and only the staples remember you.

Go to Him or go to Hell.

Those are the only two choices, because Hell will be wherever He is not.

Christ on the cross: My God, my God, why have you forsaken me?

That was exile far greater than any Hell-bound soul will ever experience. The Son, one God with the Father, experiencing divorce, separation from grace, left only with the filth, with incest and murder, malice and genocide. Left with pride and envy, left with every self-righteous glance and resentful thought. Left with the rags and rot that every soul uses to fill that God-shaped hole.

Someone had to carry it all to Hell.

I know little, but I know this: When you have died and your leaves have been raked, when you have looked on the face of God and had your final conversation, exchanging words others may never know, you will be where you want to be. If you cannot let go of yourself, if you cling to the filth that you've loved for so long, stroking the cherished scabs that line your soul—hates and bitternesses that you cannot lay down, an imagined mirror picturing a glorious self—then He will push you away. You will be sent out into the darkness, far from His presence. You will not like the darkness, but the other option seems worse. You couldn't bear to be without those scabs.

You will be in good company, wandering with preachers, priests, and kings, and every lofty human unable to live without themselves. Many "righteous" will crowd into that corner with you, people who cannot imagine themselves as anything other than good, who cannot bend to a God who will not bend to them.

Other people. And their music.

You will be exiled from joy, but you will not want it at its price. You will be exiled from love, because love means sacrifice, and why should you do that? You will be exiled from the dance, from the music, from the center stage and life in the sun.

But you will hear only thundering and clamor, you will see only blisters and work and burning pain.

If you want to love Him, then He has already begun giving you change. He has already begun unclenching your fists, taking your filth to be laundered on the cross. He is spitting in the dust and making mud to bathe your eyes. Your crippled soul will pick up its mat and walk. He will lead you down the path and through the whale's belly. On the other side, you will stand up straight, remade.

Bend your neck. Do not mourn the leaves. Do not mourn the tree.

But be warned: here the company is low and classless. Here are the whores and thieves, the deviants and the downtrodden, the slaves, the unbeautiful, the lumpy, the people who look bad in suits. Even Christians.

Here are the people who knew their own worth.

Would you go to Heaven? There is a sign you must stand beside where the man with the cigarette takes the tickets. There is a height you must achieve.

You must be wretched. That is your ticket and your only qualification. It is an unexclusive ride, but wild, with weather you've never seen, and deafening light. Perhaps unsafe.

C. S. Lewis (from *The Four Loves*): "'Is it easy to love God?' asks an old author. 'It is easy,' he replies, 'to those who do it.'"

Rory, my son, stands in his cousin's backyard and stares at the world through five-year-old eyes.

Two years later he is thinking of Grandpa Marty.

His cousin is playing while Rory examines the trees and the ground beneath his feet.

He cannot think of a way to express himself, and so he takes out the wallet we gave him to hold ice cream money from his grandmothers. He takes out his dollars and throws them in the grass.

"They're not important," he says, and shrugs, blinking.

He's right.

I help him pick them up.

Paper and ink are not important. Wealth is unimportant next to souls. So are legs and fingers, all five senses. So is life.

But gratitude is all-important. Everything is a gift. Every smell, every second, every ice cream dollar. Gratitude for the whole story, from beginning to end, gratitude for the valleys and the shadows that lead us to the novel's final page.

Take a step and thank God, for He holds you in His hand. Never ask to be put down. Never struggle for separation or for worth apart from His gifts. Breathe, taste His world, His words, and marvel that you are here to feel the blowing swirl of life. To be blown by it.

Enjoy your ice cream.

God is perfect. Justice and mercy are not abstractions; they originate in Him. They are adjectives. Every dead soul sees His face. Every soul will stand before Him and bend or clutch before

He sorts. There will be no ignorant. We do not need to look over His shoulder. We cannot. We do not know which sinners look to the cross and which choose to hang on their own.

We can only trust.

And bend.

We can laugh as we yellow. We can hold out our fingers and watch how the sun glows on our decay. We can feel the wind coming, our stems shivering and then severing. We can clutch, or we can float and tumble and wait to be raked and gathered. Let the children play on us, let them roll and jump, and we can cling to their hair, old and dying.

They will put us in the ground.

I walk with my son up the golden tunnel, kicking leaves, swirling cast-off life up to our knees.

"Lots of leaves," Rory says. Sprawling gold lands on his head and slides to his shoulder.

"Yep."

He quick-shuffles forward, mounding a crunching season against his legs. "God knows every one."

"Yes He does."

"Is that funny?"

"Yes it is."

Beethoven, struggling with deafness through most of his life, stormy and suicidal, while he lay dying of lead poisoning: "I shall hear in heaven. Clap now, my friends, the comedy is done."

Or,

Beethoven died in a thunderstorm, with a foul expression on his face, shaking an angry fist at the skies.

There are other versions.

At the top of the street, my son and I stop and turn. I crouch beside him. We look down through the tunnel; we watch the sun slant through the first golden pomp of death. The earth falls away before us, ready for the harvest.

There are many of us floating in the air, kicked along the ground, many of us riding the sunlight, painted with its life, imitating its color.

At the end of the tunnel, at the other end of history, on the corner of the block where the basalt wall and the trees end, there is a church, small and freshly painted white.

Soon we will be old and sparkly.

THE STORY

Tonight the autumn will blizzard. The trees will cast off the last of this year's many skins, and in the morning I will look at their naked forms, bristled against a gray sky. In the morning I will look at winter, but the ground will not be white. It will be blanketed with the wet colors of fire.

There are times when autumn comes graciously—as it has in the past weeks—when it acts its age and sheds slowly, when the leaf pile grows day by day until the kids can all disappear simultaneously into the barrow I have raked for them. But tonight the wind is blowing, slinging heavy water, and the maple flame along my street, my tunnel arching over the old stone wall, will be beaten down in one climactic action.

I will watch with a flashlight, like a man beside a deathbed. I have loved this season, this time; I have stood with it in the bright days and the easy days. Now, as its hands grow cold and its fires die, I will hum to it and tell it stories and swear to keep its memory.

I will watch the death rattle, and when the season is gone and stripped bones line the street, I will make chocolate hot, and I will drink it, laughing with my wife, eager for snow, for the completeness of this death, eager for this new cold to be broken by the explosive laughter of Christmas.

In the beginning there was no earth, no air, no fire, and no water. There were no up quarks or down quarks. There were no leptons or nuclei.

There were no oysters, no fat rabbits, no fast rabbits, and no falcons.

No one had invented sperm. No one had invented man or woman, magnetism, cows, or milk that can be turned to cheese, or canes excreting sweetness to be mixed with cream.

There were no green things to harvest the air with sunlight, because there was no air, no sun, no green.

There were no aphids or ants to defend them.

Wings had not yet been dreamt. Rivers had not yet been sung. Desert sand had not yet been spread and rippled.

There was no such thing as color—the behavior of light in response to a material thing.

There was no such thing as smell—the interpretation of matter by an airborne sampling.

There was no touch—the physical sensation of contact between two material things.

There was no sight—not of our sort.

No taste.

No ears.

No time.

But there was a Being, spirit, infinite, I AM. In that being there was One, and there were Many. There was Love. There was Joy. There was true Laughter. There was a Word, a Voice. There was Artist, but there was not yet art.

And that Voice said Light, and extended Himself a finite canvas to paint the only thing that could be worth painting, to paint the I AM.

The art has a beginning—it began when time did—but it will have no end. Only endings. Even now it still grows and expands, twists and interwines, rises and sets, spins and doubles back.

The Voice will never be silent.

Ants are easy to describe. They have six legs. But what words do I have to capture the transcendent? The truest description I conceive is sure to have a false side. Which of these twenty-six letters should I use to try and shape you a bust of the Infinite?

Shall I tell you a poem about footprints in the sand?

Should we talk about spheres, about spinning, about war, about philosophy, about children and insects and soil and tombstones and stars and antimatter? It is not enough.

When the Artist set Himself to this same task, naked mole rats happened. So did haiku, Saturn's rings, the three forms of water, fire, Greek people, and the occasional egg-laying mammal.

This is a task that God Himself cannot complete. He is infinite (along with all that really means—if only we really knew), and so His canvas is forever expanding. He must add extra dimensions, using the narrative arcs of single watts of energy in solar flares on suns that we won't so much as glimpse until we've laid a few thousand human histories end to end and cubed them. And He must use ants, every ant, in every yard and sidewalk crack and hole and jungle. He needed to multiply mediums as He grasped for the ungraspable, and so this is music and sculpture, this is realism, impressionism, mysticism, and above all, fantasy.

See the world as a limerick, as an epic poem, as a car commercial, as opera, as a Russian novel adapted into a pop-up book for children.

See the insects. See the desert fairy shrimp. See the stars. See Rome.

See its bones.

This is not a nonsense project. God is not questing for a square circle, looking for fertile offspring from a barren geometric breeding pair. He is not trying to speak Himself a rock so big that He can't lift it.

He is the rock He can't lift. He is the Infinite struggling to capture Himself, to reveal every facet of His Infinite Self in the limitations of tiny finite space.

He would fail if there were a time limit. He would fail if He stopped and said the piece was done. If He ever finished.

But He will never finish. As long as the Triune Three remain, paint will be mixed on the palette.

This is the only true challenge for the Infinite. Anything else is as easy as speaking. This is the only struggle for the Infinite, the only resistance He will ever meet.

The best of all possible tasks for the best of all possible Beings.

I look at the world, and I understand the impulse of some of the mystics through Christendom's odd and spotty past. I understand why they could feel the need to sit on poles for years on end or to fast to the point of death. It is a way of staring at the world without blinking, an attempt at getting at new layers long buried beneath the distractions of our flesh, our communities, our perceived needs. I understand their impulse, because sometimes I think I would understand reality better if I only ever looked at it through a toilet paper tube.

Take-Home Project (requirements: one human): In all that you do, perfectly image God.

Alternative for Struggling Students (requirements: one human hair, one eucalyptus throat lozenge): moisten hair on tongue, use it to sculpt lozenge into a comprehensive, twelve-sided frieze of history; omit no individual; include alternative theories for the origin of this universe; make especial use of ants.

We can't see everything, and we can't describe everything that we can see—not even through this small cardboard tube. But there is enough that we can.

The Infinite speaks us. We are in the frame, playing our role alongside the ants and the moss and Orion. We fell away, and our world fell with us. He stoops for us, and in the end our running and our suiciding will only picture the depth of His love, His humility. It magnifies His ultimate triumph.

Greek philosophers played their role. Plato made rules that enabled God to blaspheme, to defile Himself when He embraced the matter in His art.

To the Greeks, matter was a corruption of spirit. The immaterial was ideal, the spirit world was untainted. Flesh brought odors, needs, wrinkles, and vast storehouses of limitation.

Flesh—that curse.

And so, like John the Baptist preparing the way, the Greeks set the stage for a reversal.

The Apostle Paul could talk to them about the Infinite Word, the Spirit Creator.

Ἐν ἀρχῇ ἦν ὁ Λόγος—this could get those beards nodding; it could be crammed into their Plato picture.

But Christmas—to the Greeks, Christmas was filth, a vulgarity in the extreme.

They were right.

And thus the beauty.

If the Maker of the world were to descend to earth, how would you expect Him? If you heard that the Infinite, the Spirit Creator was entering into His own Art, wouldn't you look to the clouds? Wouldn't you look to the cherubim in their storms; wouldn't you expect a tornado chariot? I would, and in my defense, I think my sensibilities are good and entirely in the right place. It is God who is gauche.

And thus the surprise.

The Jews were waiting on a Messiah. They were waiting on a man to throw off the oppressor, someone like Judah Maccabee, someone like the King David. The Messiah came, and not just to the Jews. He did come like Judah, like David, but not how He was expected.

He came to be humbled. He came to die.

Plan the event. Arrange the reception. The King of kings is coming. He will shoulder governments. He will be called the Prince of Peace, Wonderful Counselor.

Plato, no covering your eyes, no throwing up in indignation, no offended boycotts of the crucifix set in urine. The Lord of all reality is coming to your hemisphere. And He, the pure Spirit, will take on flesh and need to eat and breathe and move His bowels, and have His diaper changed.

Don't look at me. I had plenty of glorious ideas. The blasphemy isn't mine.

He will be a carpenter, with splintered and blistered hands and cracking nails. One of His grandmothers was a whore of Jericho. He will enter the womb of a virgin and expand in the normal way. He will exit her womb in the normal way. And then she will suckle Him as the cows do their calves. Because, well, He will be mammal.

These days, we dress the whole thing up and hum until it all seems holy. We set up little plastic scenes in our yards and then we backlight them.

If God is pleased, it is because they are trite and silly—entirely in keeping with the whole event.

The Lord came to clean the unclean. He brought the taint of Holiness, and it has been growing ever since. He was born in a barn and slept in a food trough.

Maybe the livestock all took gentle knees, cognizant and pious, like in the back page of a children's Christmas book.

Maybe they smacked on their cuds and continued to lift their tails and muck in the stalls.

The angels knew what was going on even if no one else did. They grasped the bizarre reality of Shakespeare stepping onto the stage, of God making Himself vulnerable, dependent, and human—making Himself Adam. And so, in a more appropriate spirit, they arranged a concert and put on what was no doubt the greatest choral performance in planetary history.

Were the kings gathered? Where were the people with the important hats? Where were the ushers, the corporate sponsors?

The Heavenly Host, the souls and angels of stars, descended

into our atmosphere and burst in harmonic joy above a field and some rather startled shepherds.

But the crowd was bigger than that. The shepherds were a distinct minority. Mostly, the angels were just singing to sheep.

I'm sure *those* animals paid attention, and not just because there was a baby in their food bowl.

Sidenote: Does this sound like something a human would make up? Does it sound like something a bunch of cult builders would create to impress potential tithers?

And then the Holy One, the World-Maker, was born in a . . . in . . . uh . . .

And the angels themselves descended, overflowing with jubilation and sang to a randomly selected flock of sheep and a couple of their unwashed, illiterate shepherds—the Lord Incarnate's first worshippers.

Extra Sidenote: Did those sheep reproduce? Do they have lineal descendants? Is someone shearing one now and taking a basket of wool to the little boy who lives down the lane?

I'm betting it's a black sheep.

If I could get a sweater made from the wool of the descendant of one of the first Christmas sheep, would it itch like any other sweater? Would it give me visions?

Someone is wearing one now. If they only knew, it might just explain the dreams.

The reversals in the story didn't stop at Christ's birth. Rather than being celebrated, one of the first plot elements was Herod's declaration of genocide. The King of kings is here, you say? Bathe the land in infant blood.

Slaughter, Rachel weeping for her children lost . . . these things are part of the Christmas story. For some reason, we leave the soldiers, dead babies, and weeping mothers out of the plastic figurine collection.

Herod, the first king to fall, was eaten by worms. Where is he now? Where is the matter he used to use?

The infant Israel was taken by night into Egypt and escaped that early death.

Whom did Christ fight? The leaders of His own religion, His professed management. The righteous.

What did Christ do in the temple? He whipped people and flipped tables. Later He even ripped that big, expensive purple curtain.

With whom did He sit and eat? Whores. Thieves. The unclean.

From birth to the end, He never left the trough. Christ walked from insult to insult, from filth to filth.

Lepers. Prostitutes. Tax men. The Dead.

He chose fishermen to stand closest to Him, and from among the educated He chose one great man—a murderer who didn't want to come and had to be knocked off his donkey.

How would He conquer? When would He leave this path of uncleanness?

He came to be stripped naked. He came to be lashed. He came to have His beard ripped out and thorns rammed onto His head. He came to be mocked, to have His body pierced with rough-forged nails and a Roman spear. To be severed from His father and experience Hell as Adam—for man.

He came to live in the trough and die on a pole.

Pilate, you conversed with your Maker. Truth stood in front of you, and you asked Him, "What is truth?"

Pilate, you have had another conversation. What words did you have?

The Word has shown how far He can stoop. From the pole, He went into the ground. From the ground, He went deeper, all the way to Tartarus, beating out a path for those coming behind, for the thief who walked beside Him.

The whale did not spit Him up. He ripped the whale open. The stone was rolled away.

The Guards: Priests, the Christ was no liar. He has come again.

The Priests: Take this money. Tell no one.

Members of the Sanhedrin, there has been another trial. What was your defense? Even the sheep can testify against you.

◆

In the cold, I stand, shivering in the dark storm, moving my light up and down my tunnel. It is collapsing in a rush. These leaves aren't fluttering; they aren't spinning on sun-gold air. They are dying swiftly in the night, their colors already hidden.

I see Rome falling, collapsed by rain.

I see Byzantium, with the pomp of great hats and the importance of emperors.

I see China in confusion.

I see Africa slipping to the earth.

I see Nietzsche and Plato, Hume and Leibniz and Kant. I see kings and prophets unable to stand.

I see myself, my people, my country, my leaves, my blood.

We are dying. We must die. The road is well traveled. We need not fear the dark, for the way is lit with Christmas lights.

We go into the ground, where the moss will feed on us and others will be stacked on top. We go into church floors and graveyards behind grocery stores. We go into the sea and the snow. We are devoured—by each other, by the earth, by time, by cancers and confusion, by the spinning of this sphere as it runs its balanced laps.

We are in Winter, where the light dies and blood runs cold.

But we are not forgotten. Wet, ripped from the trees and trampled, we will not be lost, for we are His words, and when His voice calls, we will come.

Offstage, there is another greater stage.

Come, let us grow old like fishermen. Let us sweeten the air with songs while we fade. Let us die. Winter cannot hold us. Let us go into the ground, and our faces will find the sun. Let us ride the eruption of Easter.

Our Maker waits. He would have a conversation. What words will we have?

We need only one, the One who spoke us.

We will hear the angels sing. We will be the sheep. We will be made new and find ourselves standing in a garden. We will be handed bodies and shovels and joy.

No tree will be prohibited.

Blister your hands. Tend to the ants. Push the shadows back. Sing. Make a garden of the world.

We will laugh and carve Finis on the earth. We will carve it on the moon. We will look to the Voice, to the Singer, the Painter, the Poet, the One born in a barn, the One with holes in His hands and oceans in His eyes, and on *that* day we will know—

The story has begun.

And we will rake the leaves.

Finis

GRATITUDE

There are people and things in need of acknowledgment.

I'd like to thank insects everywhere for all that they do, and the BBC for producing *Life in the Undergrowth* (and enabling me to spend more time in the world of exoskeletons). I also owe gratitude to Annie Dillard for the texture in her voice, and to Nietzsche, for being the only philosopher to make me laugh out loud. My debt to C. S. Lewis and G. K. Chesterton should be obvious to any who know them. Thanks also to Herbert Lockyer for *Last Words of Saints and Sinners*, and to many other unnamed writers who have seasoned me.

I owe thanks to a regiment of teachers and professors who tried to shovel things into my head and generally put up with me through my years in their classrooms. Their effort was noble, and they should not be held accountable for the result.

I am profoundly indebted to my wife, my mother, and my father. They've set my feet and shaped my vision. More than that, they've read this, and they're still nice to me.

Thanks also to Thomas Nelson, and to my editor and publisher for being willing to publish an . . . abnormal book. And thanks to my children (Rory, Lucia, Ameera, and Seamus) for jumping on my back whenever they feel the need.

Thank you for spinning with me, for sharing in the dizziness, and for making it this far. Assuming, of course, that you got this far through the traditional means and not by villainously flipping to the end first. If you are a to-the-end-flipper, then my thoughts about you are dark and my feelings do not involve gratitude.

But whether you are a reader or a flipper, you are here now, and I have something for you, something to remind you that you are on a sphere, hurtling in circles while it spins, something to remind you of what you're made of, where you live, and how soon you'll be gone. A token of my gratitude:

TJIT

Lick the word and press the page against the back of your hand. You're a little wiser now, because now you know what ink tastes like in a paperback.

Show the carnies, and they might even let you back on the rides.

As for me, well, the lights are still bright and the corners are still dark, but I have fallen off of one ride already. It is time to stagger into the night.

ABOUT THE AUTHOR

N. D. Wilson is a best-selling author, professional day-dreamer, and occasional screenwriter. His novels include the 100 Cupboards trilogy and the Ashtown Burials series. He also has several scripts in various stages of development. He enjoys hilltops, calluses, and the smell of rain on hot asphalt. He and his wife have five children, and they watch them battle the sea with surfboards and buckets as often as possible. He once faked the Shroud of Turin, which got him yelled at on Hungarian television, and he typed a tiny novel on a paper napkin which was then printed in *Esquire* magazine (that bastion of righteous-ness). He is currently a Fellow of Literature at New Saint Andrews College, where he teaches freshmen how to play with words. Like everyone else, he is made from dust.

OTHER BOOKS BY N. D. WILSON:

Death by Living

Leepike Ridge

100 Cupboards

Dandelion Fire